Cyclone Devastation: Its Implications

CYCLONE DEVASTATION: ITS IMPLICATIONS

Dr. K. VIJAYA KUMAR
Associate Professor of Sociology
School of Distance Education
Andhra University
Visakhapatnam, AP.

SERIALS PUBLICATIONS
New Delhi

First Published–2005

ISBN: 81-86771-60-3

Published by

Head Office : **SERIALS PUBLICATIONS**
4, B.S.S. Hall, Khyber Pass Market,
Civil Lines, Delhi–110054 (India)
Fax: 91-11-23812678
Phone: 23245225
e-mail: serials@satyam.net.in

Branch Office : *4830/24, Prahlad Street, Ansari Road,*
Darya Ganj, New Delhi-110002 (India)

Printed at :

PRINTED IN INDIA

DEDICATION

To

The Cyclone Victims of
Coastal Andhra Pradesh, India

Foreword

The Book Covers some important aspects relating to Cyclone devastation along with relevant rehabilitation and reconstruction programmes, suggesting modification in the implementation of the said programmes.

To improve the quality of life among the cyclone affected victims, effective implementation methods of rehabilitation and reconstruction operations are indicated, thereby imbibing awareness and alertness to native population in facing natural disasters through literacy campaigns which will be more useful to native people along with local bureaucrats to tide over the disaster crisis and take safeguards for themselves, along with facing life threat of the public. This book will be useful for the government and the public alike, in the context of a devastation - plagued social situation.

This work is empirical and based on primary data, therefore it will be used for further research for exploring new pathways.

I trust this book will also be useful as a valuable document for the professionals and the laymen alike.

Y.C. SIMHADRI
Vice-Chancellor
Andhra University
Visakhapatnam
Andhra Pradesh

Foreword

The Book Covers some important aspects relating to Cyclone devastation along with relevant rehabilitation and reconstruction programmes, suggesting modifications in the implementation of the said programmes.

To improve the quality of life among the cyclone affected victims, effective implementation methods of rehabilitation and reconstruction operations are indicated, thereby imbibing awareness and alertness in the population in facing natural disasters through literacy campaigns which will be more useful to utilise people along with local functionaries to tide over the flux of crisis and take safeguards for themselves, along with forming the thread of the public. This book will be useful for the government and the public alike, in the context of a devastation prone social situation.

This work is empirical and based on primary data. I hope it will be used for further research for exploring new pathways.

I am confident this book will also be useful as a valuable document for the professionals and the laymen alike.

Y.C. SIMHADRI
Vice-Chancellor
Andhra University
Visakhapatnam
Andhra Pradesh

Acknowledgements

I place on record my sincere and unconditional acknowledgement to Dr. Y.S. Rajasakhar Reddy, Honorable Chief Minister of A.P. for the inspiration I drew from his efforts to serve the depressed people of our state.

I wish to express my deep sense of gratitude to our beloved Vice-Chancellor, Prof. (Dr.) Y.C. Simhadri who extended co-operation and moral support to me as a well-wisher during my academic career.

I thank the Collector and all the officials of East Godavari District for having supplied official information relating to the research project.

I thank Dr. S. Vanaja Rani, project fellow who has sincerely attended to her work.

I thank my field assistants, Ch. Bhaskara Rao, A. Durga Prasad, DVSSNS Sharma, and VSVS Narayana Murthy for their attentive field-work.

I thank Kirla Krishna Rao who extended his full co-operation by giving me relevant information as and when required.

I thank all the respondents who gave us information whenever asked for in spite of their suffering.

I thank Mr. P. Samuel Paul and Dr. S. Sree Ram Murthy who always gave their assistance whenever required by me.

I thank to Ch.V.V. Sita Ram Reddy his attentive typing work.

I thank the University Grants Commission for providing the requisite funding for the project.

Finally, I express my deep sense of gratitude to the School of Distance Education, Andhra University for facilitating my work during the project period.

Preface

It is generally known that a cyclone, when fully developed, in a vast Whirlwind of extraordinary violence, 150 to 800 km. across and 10 to 17 km. high, spiralling around 300 to 500 km, a day. The winds associated with such storms are among the most violent and the rainfall accompanying them, is always very heavy.

The cyclone under study, which struck the East Coast during the period from 6th to 9th November 1996, contains all the ingredients of a havoc-ridden disaster. As an area of its impact, the central delta in East Godavari District is chosen to understand the sociological implications of the post-cyclone period.

The study is undertaken to cover five mandals of Amalapuram Revenue Division, selecting villages on a random basis.

As can be seen in this cyclone also, there are many similarities of other cyclones which had their impact on the low-lying area, of the coastal belt.

As every cyclone tests the integrity of the preparedness of the people and the officials, this cyclone of November 1996 has its own version of havoc throwing a challenge for containing the impact on the people and the administrators alike.

Dr. K. Vijaya Kumar

Contents

1

Introduction

India is endowed with a long coastline of over 8,000 km. and has a variety of natural coastal ecosystems. The Eastern Coast is low-lying with lagoons, marshes, beaches and deltas while the Western Coast is dominated by rocky shores. The islands of Lakshadweep like those of Maldives, are composed of atolls while the Andamans and Nicobar islands arise from a submerged mountain chain, and are volcanic in origin. Coastal areas of the country are shelter to some of the richest, most diverse and fragile natural resources. Coastal habitats like mangroves serve to protect the coasts, prevent coastal erosion and mitigate the effects of natural disasters like cyclones, typhoons and tidal waves. These ecosystems help stabilize the physical environment by dissipating the wave action by buffeting salinity changes and by stabilizing sediments. Coastal population depend on mangrove-related resources for their socio-economic needs such as fuel and fisheries as well as for other byproducts like honey, timber, tannin, coal, fruit and fodder. Of late, there has been a significant increase in eco-tourism, aquaculture and agriculture in mangrove protected areas (MPA). Although these activities do yield economic gains for the coastal people, the mangrove ecosystem itself is under threat in certain areas due to aquaculture and developmental activities. However, the rich coastal habitats of India are being threatened among other things by pollution especially from land-based sources, "development" projects such as ports and big dams, irresponsible tourism, deforestation, natural disasters, overfishing and destructive fishing practices. Expansion of human activities especially of a commercial nature have also led to excessive withdrawal of groundwater in the fragile coastal belt and many parts of the coastline are being threatened by salinity incursions (The Hindu: Survey of Environment, 1997).

The concept of growth at all costs which governed development policies around the world until the eighties, is being replaced in the Nineties by the idea of sustainable development. This is the consequence of growing evidence of the heavy price we have to pay for unsustainable consumption patterns particularly of the richer countries.

In the name of growth, fossil fuels have been burnt, chemicals harmful to the atmosphere have proliferated, poisons have been dumped on land and in rivers and in oceans and natural resources such as forests have been ravaged and exploited to the point of near extinction. As a result, we are confronted with the phenomenon on of "global warming", caused by accumulation of gases such as carbon dioxide in the atmosphere, and the depletion of the ozone layer. Some of the possible environmental changes associated with global warming are hot dry summers exceptional drought or rainfall, floods, storms, tidal surges, water stagnation and eutrophication.

The coastal stretches of peninsular India are much prone to cyclones that originate in the high reaches of the Bay of Bengal and Arabian Sea. The Ocean depressions coupled with North-East and South-West monsoons cause much devastation to the coastal economic zone. Such a natural calamity generally takes place during August - November in a year.

Andhra Pradesh is India's third largest State with a population of 66 millions, 1991 census and larger than most of the nations. Almost half of Andhra Pradesh's population live in the eight districts of the coastal belt. The coastal districts of Andhra Pradesh experience cyclonic devastation almost every year due to its geographical position in relation to the Bay of Bengal, ocean currents and wind paths. The entire coastal stretch gets hit by the cyclones and its allied natural stretches like the deltas of the rivers Godavari, Krishna and Pennar which are much prone to great losses both in terms of lives and materials. Since the delta region lies low with monotonous landscape, even the low magnitude of cyclones causes much devastation. The deltas of the coastal regions are providing two eco-niches such as aquatic and inland resources. The former resource is exploited by the fishing communities, while the latter is utilised by the agrarian communities. The settlements of the fishing population are located, as is natural, very contiguous to the coast. Annually, one or two cyclonic storms either hit or skirt the Andhra coast, some in April-May and in September-December May. The months October and November are statistically the critical months. The most vulnerable coastal districts are: Krishna, Prakasam, Guntur, East Godavari and West Godavari. These are all low lying and most of the mandals contain heavily populated delta areas. A storm surge is likely to sweep inland, if it strikes any of these districts and the areas are also subject to flooding from inland rain.

Statement of the Problem

In the reckon of the recent cyclone devastation on the East Coast of Andhra Pradesh, it is proposed to undertake a sociological survey on the effects of cyclone. The study examines Sociological, Social-Psychological and Economical conditions of the people of East Godavari District before and after the cyclone that has occurred during 6-8, November 1996. For all practical purposes, this study will be referred to as "Cyclone Devastation in Andhra Pradesh".

Table 1.1: District-wise details of cyclones in A.P. during the past 100 years.

Sl. No.	*District Cycloness*	*Number of severe*	*Number of cyclones with Cyclones*	*Number of cyclones with wind speed >100 km*	*Number of total wave height > 5 km.*
1.	Nellore	20	9	3	3
2.	Prakasam	10	3	2	2
3.	Krishna	18	9	5	5
4.	Guntur	—	—	—	—
5.	West Godavari	—	—	—	—
6.	East Godavari	8	2	2	2
7.	Visakhapatnam	3	2	1	1
8.	Vizianagaram	—	—	—	—
9.	Srikakulam	10	4	2	2
Total:		**69**	**29**	**15**	**15**

Source: CWC, Visakhapatnam.

As the cyclonic storm crossed the coast-line (known as landing of tidal surge), the cyclonic wind which moved in circular motion at a speed ranging from 80 - 221 kmph (or 250 kmph) and the storm surge creating its impact inside the land, created devastating effects. The consequent effects of heavy rains associated with high wind velocity were: (a) The entire area of Konaseema was covered with full of fallen, broken, uprooted coconut trees; (b) Telephone poles, electric poles were damaged and twisted with wires; (c) There was debris of buildings and houses, along with animal carcasses, here and there; (d) Several people died in some places like Balusutippa and Bhyravapalem areas. (e) There were no communication and transportation facilities and the area was cut off from the mainland and it led to total paralysis of normal human life. The cyclone storm crossed the coast at Kakinada at 10.30 p.m. about 50 km in the North-West direction on the 6th day of November 1996. Despite all steps taken by the authorities,

The cyclone washed away the entire Village, shattered it into ruins

The coconut tree fallen across a road blocking up the traffic during the cyclone

A sad view of victimized fishermen at the coast during the cyclone

A great burden to the villagers fetching the water from a far away place because of water nearby their village being salty and polluted by the rubbish during the cyclone period

the storm has devasted both the Central and Eastern deltas in the district in an unprecedented manner.

Thousands of trees were uprooted, thatched houses were completely damaged and the entire socio-economic infrastructure was damaged.

The unpredicted nature, when lashed its fury in the disctrict, resulted in the loss of great number of lives. As people lay dismayed by the fear of howling sounds of strong winds, they stayed indoors, and the hurricane winds lashed at some villages for more than 10 continuous hours. The cyclone crushed thousands who lay injured, crying for medical help and rescue which was not available, with transportation and communication problems. The twisted poles were tangled with wires, the roads were breached and covered with uprooted trees. Several villages were inaccessible and the magnitude of the disaster could not be accurately assessed so far.

The houses of thousands of families were evacuated, except from concrete roofing houses, which escaped the fury of cyclone. At the same time, all tiled houses and thatched houses were blown away. A very few trees managed to stay unhurt. The rest of the trees were wildly chapped out and uprooted. The paddy, banana, coconut, vegetables, chilli and tobacco were completely damaged in lakhs of acres. The economy of the region suffered a big blow.

The Konaseema is a renowned region for its unsurpassing beauty. But today, it is a picture of wailing atmosphere. People, along with cattle lost their lives and the houses and trees lost their living appearance. No longer, Konaseema is an attractive spot of the State but instead looks glum with traces of a graveyard.

Isolation, insecurity and disruption of transportation, along with communication networks, have created vacuum in one's family, neighbourhood and the environment. Thus, a person who is left in the wilderness in that melancholic life, makes him/her diffident and socially lonesome.

Death of everyone in the family, except himself, makes a respondent shockingly lonely and makes him with a feeling of loss, making him incompetent to face life single-handedly. The deadly scenario makes him exhausted, weak and diffident, leading to psychotrauma and maladjustment including premature death, following the natural calamity.

Agricultural fields after the havoc, were not in a fit condition to cultivate as there is no distinction between land and water, with the whole area inundated, all looking like a big pool. Stagnated water for a day left the land infertile. Many fishing villages were washed away with many boats and nets lost to the vagaries of nature.

The devastation pushed the people in a helpless condition, owing to lack of basic items of food, clothing, drinking-water and medicines etc., to meet the day-to-day needs. Added to this, there was sudden skyrocketing of prices of essential goods, thereby creating scarcity of day-to-day rations and thereby pushing the middle and upper class persons to lower class levels, which is a shocking experience, inculcating both psychological and sociological dimensions. A study of such a socio-economic downfall is necessary, while planning for rehabilitation and reconstruction programmes.

Review of Literature

It is Paradoxical that research done or studies made in this vital area of frequent cyclone-caused disasters are limited (See, for instance: Morris-Jones: 1964; Brahma and Gole: 1966; Lifton: 1969; Chen: 1973; Mathur and Bhattacharya: 1975; Vijayalakshmi: 1977; Reddy: 1977; Cunny et al: 1978; Menon: 1978; Ivan Fera: 1978; Subrahmanyam: 1978; and Cohen and Raghavulu: 1979). As such literature generated is scanty and sporadic, throwing limited light on the subject. This is basically due to the fact that such natural disasters occur too infrequently to warrant a great attention from the social scientists to study and investigate the situation. Such research activity in this regard is intermittent, since the number of natural disasters has been slowly decreasing and their geographical locations remaining, dispersed. Also, different kinds of natural disasters present different problems for studying their socio-economic and politico-administrative implications, thereby providing little scope for generalization and theorization. The consequence of which is that these studies are basically atheoretical and generally descriptive in nature, shying away from the theory and methodology, and focusing on only the problems of relief and rehabilitation offered to the victims.

However, the critical variable in much of this havoc, as suggested by the review of literature available is of course, the social system. How the social system perceives and responds to an impending disaster is vital both in terms of the immediate situation and its long-term implications.

The most important areas that are yet to be covered scientifically in this vital field of disaster research, as identified by the present researcher, are the role of private groups and voluntary organizations in the relief process; the magnitude of resources available to the State and the local authorities; the attitude of these authorities towards outside help; the role of bureaucracy in rushing relief; the inchoate system of allocating Central resources and assistance; the pervasive role of short-term political calculations; the role of intermediaries, pressure groups and non-affected people in taking advantage of the situation and grabbing the resources and finally the corrupting influence of symbolic crusaders on the actual relief and rehabilitation process. All these issues need detailed investigation in the context of a devastation-plagued social situation.

Ideally speaking disaster relief and rehabilitation work should be a co-operative activity in which four different categories of participants namely survivors, bureaucrats, political leaders and voluntary organizations should work together. But unfortunately, in many instances, it is our suspicion and guess that the activities of one category either overlap one another or come into clash with others in the role-set. But such an overlap or clash of interests in this sphere would reflect on the performance level and gives negative effect. Further, if any of these participants have very high expectations concerning the others and if these expectations are not fulfilled, we can again predict difficulty. This problem would be compounded by the politicization of the relief and rehabilitation effort. Also, in such a situation, the intermediaries will emerge between the survived victims and the relief and rehabilitation apparatus. Unfortunately, all these aspects are not yet studied adequately and scientifically and the present researcher feels about it as a gap in the existing knowledge.

The main purpose of the present study is therefore to assess the physical and social impact of the cyclone, along with its economic and political consequences and to analyze the patterns of individual and institutional responses to the event. All this would help, it is hoped in developing suitable programmes for containing the problem under investigation covering the target area.

The emergence of non-affected people taking advantage of devastation in the early days, which is very rare. But after sometime, the non-affected people may be allured or tempted by intermediatory persons to claim benefits on par with the victims.

The following are the assumptions under which the non-affected people may take advantage of devastation: (a) Non-affected people get tempted to claim the doles/benefits provided to the victims as their socio-economic conditions motivate to claim; (b) There may be a scope for common understanding between local bureaucrats/local petty officers and non-affected people; (c) The politicians and some other pressure groups, who may extend their support in favour of their party sympathizers for providing all benefits to the non-victims to gain personal popularity and strengthen their political base, by diluting the real spirit of relief and rehabilitation programmes; (d) On some occasions, the losses which may be exaggerated, may take place for more benefits.

Study Area

The study is conducted in one of the coastal districts of Andhra Pradesh viz., East Godavari, one of the most vulnerable coastal districts which is subjected to frequent spell of cyclones rooted in the Bay of Bengal.

Aim of the Project

The study will be operated in one of the coastal districts of Andhra Pradesh namely East Godavari, which is subjected to frequent spells of cyclones rooted in the Bay of Bengal.

Objectives of the Study

1. To ascertain the natural extent and magnitude of the devastation caused by the November 1996 cyclone,
2. To analyse the sociological social-psychological and economical aspects of the study area, before and after the impact of cyclone,
3. To assess the rehabilitation programmes initiated by Government and NGOs,
4. To assess the attitudes of beneficiaries towards implementation of rehabilitation and reconstruction programmes,

5. To assess the attitudes of the Government and the NGOs towards the reconstruction programmes,
6. To suggest modifications, if any, in the impleme-ntation of the said programmes to achieve a well-desired social transformation,
7. To investigate and record carefully all the perceptions and reactions of the affected (survival victims) people during the field study.

Methodology

The rationality of the study in confining to East Godavari District is that, the cyclonic storm crossed the East Coast in the South of Kakinada, the district headquarters town, and caused heavy damages to kacha/ semi-permanent houses and crops, resulting in huge losses of life and property with disruption of communication lines and electricity supply in almost all the mandals in the district.

Out of the five Revenue Divisions in East Godavari District, Amalapuram Revenue division is selected for the study. The rationality of selecting this Revenue Division is that the extent of damage is more pronounced in Amalapuram Divisions than in other four Division in terms of damage to lives and property (see Table-1.2 and Table 1.3).

In Amalapuram Revenue Division, out of 16 mandals, five mandals are selected for study based on the extent of damages to lives and property. The selected five mandals are Amalapuram, Ambajipeta, I. Polavaram, Ainavilli and Katrenikona. In Amalapuram mandal, out of 18 villages, three villages are selected for the study. In Ambajipeta, out of 13 villages, three villages are selected. In I. Polavaram mandal, out of 11 villages, five villages are selected. In Ainavilli mandal, out of 17 villages, six villages are selected and in Katrenikona mandal, out of 14 villages, seven villages are selected. According to the notification of

Table 1.2 Extent of damage to lives and property in E.G. Dt., Nov 6th 1996.

Sl. No.	Name of the Revenue Division	(a) Deaths		(b) Missing	(c) Injured		(d) Number of Houses damaged		(e) Number of petty shops damaged	(f) Number of fishermen affected for loss of Boats, crafts etc.
		Number reported	Number identified		Seriously injured	Simple injuries	Fully	Partly		
1.	Amalapuram	832	547	837	262	512	1.58.667	65.705	8.647	11.602
2.	Rajahmundry	75	62	39	22	94	43.610	91.733	1.057	1.182
3.	Kakinada	60	48	807	—	11	55.733	24.448	488	5.806
4.	Peddapuram	6	4	—	—	—	291	2.598	—	95
5.	Rampachodavaram	5	5	—	—	—	88	234	—	—
	District Total	**978**	**666**	**1535**	**288**	**617**	**2.58.389**	**1.84.718**	**10.192**	**18.685**

(Table Contd...)

Table 1.2: Contd...

Sl. No.	*Name of the Revenue Division*	(g) Cropped-Area damaged			(h) Coconut			
		Number of villages fully affected	Total area fully damaged (sq. Km.)	Number of SF & MF fully affected	Extent involved in acres	Number of trees damaged		Number of farmers affected
1.	Amalapuram	199	52.504	1.15.027	74.034	33.92.420	23.97.650	1.94.329
2.	Rajahmundry	186	56.030	97.803	7.766	5.52.276	2.15.265	21.198
3.	Kakinada	159	47.569	66.389	9.032	4.09.763	1.94.314	17.227
4.	Peddapuram	135	9.012	21.123	—	—	—	—
5.	Rampachodavaram	61	233	449	—	—	—	—
	District Total	**740**	**1.65.348**	**3.00791**	**90.832**	**43.54.459**	**28.07.229**	**2.32.754**

the Collector, East Godavari District, a total of 215 villages in Amalapuram Revenue Division are severely affected with more than 75 per cent damage.

Table 1.3: List of villages affected by the cyclonic storm on 6th November, 1996.

Sl. No.	*Name of the Revenue Division*	*Number of villages*	*Category-I above 75% damage*	*Category-II 50% to 75% damage*	*Category-III below 50% damage*
1.	Amalapuram	215	215	—	—
2.	Rajahmundry	208	147	61	—
3.	Kakinada	161	122	39	—
4.	Peddapuram	268	—	268	—
5.	Rampachodavaram	559	—	60	499

See Table-1.3 for list of villages affected due to cyclonic storm which occurred on 6th November, 1996. The sample distribution of respondents village-wise and mandal-wise is presented in Table-1.4.

The selection of the villages is based on random sampling. Every sixth village in Amalapuram mandal is selected for the study, and every fourth village in Ambajipeta mandal is selected. In the same way, every second village in I. Polavaram mandal, every third village in Ainavilli mandal and every second village in Katrenikona mandal are selected for the study. The size of the sample is 600 and the total respondents are purposively selected, depending upon the damage, availability, convenience and responsiveness of the respondents of each village.

The data are collected by administering a pre-designed schedule consisting of structured and open-ended questions through interviews. The schedule consists of questions with regard to: (a) respondents' personal details (like age, marital status, literacy level, caste, religion, occupation, income level); (b) household particulars (like sex composition, number of earning members, their literacy,

Table 1.4: Sample Distribution.

Mandal	*Village*	*Number of Respondents*	*Mandal-wise Total Respondents "and percentages"*
Amalapuram	Bandarulanka	25	
	Peruru	26	85 (14.2)
	Sakurru	34	
Ambajipeta	Ambajipeta	30	
	Gangalakurru	23	78 (13.0)
	Tondavaram	25	
I. Polavaram	G. Moolapolam	40	
	G. Vemavaram	35	
	Muramalla	20	131 (21.8)
	T. Kottapalli	11	
	Yedurlanka	25	
Ainavilli	Ainavilli	35	
	Nallacheruvu	35	
	Nedunuru	15	163 (27.2)
	Pottilanka	28	
	Siripalli	25	
	Tottaramudi	25	
Katrenikona	Nalusutippa	40	
	Dontukurru	7	
	Kandikuppa	15	
	Katrenikona	18	143 (23.8)
	Masanitippa	5	
	Pallamkurru	45	
	Uppudi	13	
	Total	**600**	**600 (100.0)**

(Figures in parentheses indicate percentages)

occupation, income levels), (c) extent of damage to lives, property and crops; (d) time taken to restore to original position (both financial and psychological); (e) life styles, living and psychological conditions before, during and after the incidence of cyclone; (f) opinions of respondents with regard to adequacy of rehabilitation programmes at the time and after the impact of cyclone as conducted by the Central and State Governments, along with voluntary organizations; (g) the extent of damages and restoration of villages, according to respondents; (h) politicization of relief and rehabilitation effort; Using the schedule, the data are collected from 600 respondents by the field investigators.

The collected data are structured and in case of open-ended questions these were coded and tabulated by using computers.

Analysis and Interpretation

For all the variables, the data are presented mandal-wise and later the total figures are given. Statistical techniques like percentages and mean values are calculated for social, economical and psychological parameters. Interpretation for every Table is given mandal-wise in order to explain the comparisons within mandals and the overall scenario is also analysed and interpreted later. Standard techniques like cross-tables are used with regard to restoration and opinions on rehabilitation facilities while taking into consideration the variables like respondent's age, literacy level, caste, occupation, total household income etc. Finally, the data, analysis and interpretations are presented accordingly.

Chapterisation

The study consists of six chapters. The present First Chapter is Introductory and it contains the area of problem, objectives, significance, methodology, analysis, chapterization and limitations of the study. The Second Chapter deals with the profile of the study area while the profile of the sampled respondents is presented in the Third Chapter. The Fourth Chapter examines the extent of damages to lives and property, and it explains about the activities of restoration to come to original position, and about the rescue and rehabilitation facilities. Discussions about restoration and rehabilitation are made with cross-tables consisting of caste, age, literacy, occupation and total household income which are presented in the Fifth Chapter.

The final and Sixth Chapter summarises the above chapters and suggestions are given to improve the quality of life of the cyclone-affected victims by following effective implementation methods of rehabilitation and reconstruction operations to imbibe awareness and alertness to native population towards natural disasters through literacy campaigns.

Limitations

As any social study will have its own limitations, this study is no exception:

1. The first limitation is the selection of villages and respondents. The size of the sample in each village is not uniform as it is very difficult for the field investigators to do random selection of affected respondents' convenience the intensity of the problem, and the openness of the respondents are taken into account in the selection of villages and respondents.
2. Another limitation is that comparison can be made when there is previous economic status with that of the extent of damage done due to cyclone. This point is missing in this study.
3. Migration another important social factor is also not dealt with.
4. Comparisons can also be done like affected respondents with that of unaffected respondents in the same place based on their social-economic criteria or affected mandals (Revenue Divisions) with that of un-affected mandals.

In spite of the limitations the study throws a new light though sampling technique which is so far absent in this type of studies. Further, the study broadens the path to new researchers to explore further so that this can be an eye-opener to the Government in dealing with mitigation of natural disasters.

2

Profile of the Study Area

Andhra Pradesh is the fifth largest State in India, with a total population of 66 millions, (with 7.9 per cent of the total population of the Country). The sex-ratio in Andhra Pradesh is 972 females for every 1000 males. The literacy rate is 44.1 per cent, out of that, male literacy is 55.1 per cent and female literacy is 32.7 per cent. The State has a 600-mile coastline. The selected district, East Godavari is one among the 10 coastal districts of Andhra Pradesh (1991 census).

East Godavari District lies between latitudes 16° and 10°-88°, longitudes, 88°-29° and 82°37°. It is bounded on the North by Madhya Pradesh and Orissa States and on the West by Khammam and West Godavari Districts, and on the East and South by the Bay of Bengal.

The population of the district is 45,41,220 as per 1991 census, which is 6.8 per cent of the total population of the State. It is the most populous district in Andhra Pradesh. Out of the total population, males constitute 22,72,962 and females 22,68,260, with a sex ratio of 998 females per 1000 males. The geographical area of the district is 10,807 sq. km. which is only 3.9 per cent of the total area of the State, with a density of population of 420 persons per sq. km. While 23.8 per cent of the population reside in urban areas, the remaining 76.2 per cent live in rural areas. In this district, 16.3 per cent of the population are below the poverty line, and are living in rural areas and another 40.6 per cent are living in urban areas. Caste composition of the district shows that Scheduled Castes constitute 18.2 per cent of the population and Scheduled Tribes constitute 3.9 per cent. The district has total main workers of 16,68,940. Agricultural labour consist of 67.9 per cent with 5.3 per cent in industries, 3.3 per cent in cottage industries, 22.3 per cent in service sector.

The literacy rate in the district is 48.8 per cent while male literacy is 55.3 per cent and female literacy is 42.4 per cent. Rural literacy rate is 43.4 per cent and urban literacy is 65.5 per cent in this district. There are 2,760 Primary schools, with 3,79,432 of enrollment, along with 296 Upper Primary schools with 1,14,432 of enrollment, 282 High Schools with 1,20,031 enrollment and 64 Junior and Degree colleges. Besides, there are 2 Polytechnics, 2 I.T.I.s, 2 Medical Colleges and one Engineering college.

People from fishermen community are 1,05,106 living in this district. Fishing industry is a significant one in this district besides agriculture. 12,800 tonnes of sea-fish and 1,686 tonnes of inland fish account for the year 1992-93. The district has 51 Ice plants with a capacity of 351 tonnes a day, 6 freezing plants with a 25.5 tonnes capacity per day and 6 cold storages with a total capacity of 645 tonnes.

East Godavari District consists of five Revenue Divisions. Out of the five Revenue divisions, there are 59 mandals. It has a total coast-line of 161 km. and most of the mandals in the district are vulnerable to cyclone and consequential heavy rains.

Amalapuram Revenue Division is one among the five Revenue Divisions in East Godavari District. The division is an island surrounded by water on all its sides. The Gowthami Godavari River lies to its North, the Bay of Bengal is to its Eastern and Southern sides while the

Vasista River is on the Western side. It is also known as "Konaseema", which means the land situated at the end. The geographical area of the division is 3,83,176 acres (1,550.66 sq. km.) out of which the net area sown during kharif (1999-2000) is 2,59,239 acres.

The total population of the division is 11,23,922, as per 1991 census, out of which there are 5,60,540 males and 5,63,382 females. The division consists of 3,10,595 (27.6 per cent) scheduled castes and 6,941 (0.6 per cent) scheduled Tribe population. The number of educational institutions available in this division are: Schools (Primary, and Upper Primary, High Schools and A.P. Residential Schools)-1,203; Colleges (Junior and Degree)-31; Technical-12 (Polytechnic-1, I.T.Is-8, Engineering college-1, Teacher Training Institutes-2).

The main crops in the division are: paddy (1,40,482 acres), coconut (1,04,515 acres), Plantains (15,037 acres) and sugarcane (3,480 acres). The main source of irrigation is Godavari canals and the main soils in the division are alluvial making Konaseema, the Rice Bowl of the entire State of Andhra Pradesh.

Table 2.1

I. East Godavari district - Revenue Divisions

1. Amalapuram
2. Rajahmundry
3. Kakinada
4. Peddapuram
5. Rampachodavaram

Previous History of Natural Calamities in Amalapuram Division

Amalapuram Revenue Division has experienced two severe floods (one in 1953 and another in 1986) and three cyclones (1969, 1977 and 1996). Another natural hazard

Table 2.2: Table showing the particulars of population and other items in the selected mandals of Amalapuram Revenue Division, E.G. Dt.

Sl. No.	Name of the mandal	L.c. No.	Geographical area in Sq. kms	Residential houses	No. of Households	Total population Male	Female	Total
1.	Ambajipeta	48	53.92	12,877	14,247	31,662	31,640	63,302
2.	Ainavilli	49	94.30	12,251	14,398	32,501	32,681*	65,182
3.	I.Polavaram	51	128.20	12,717	15,037	33,961	33,861	67,822
4.	Katrenikona	52	135.90	13,695	15,298	35,064	34,455	69,519
5.	Amalapuram	54	80.07	14,525	17,783	37,654	38,207*	75,861
	Total		**1489.79**	**2,26,405**	**2,55,405**	**5,60,540**	**5,63,382**	**11,23,922**

from the ground called 'ONGC Blow-out' (also known as, Pasarlapudi Blow-out in the year 1995.

Table 2.3: Mandals in Amalapuram Revenue Division and extent of damage due to Nov.96 Cyclone, E.G. Dt.

Amalapuram Revenue Division

Sl. No.	*Name of Mandal*	*Number of Villages*	*Extent of damage (above 75 per cent damage)*
1.	Katrenikona	14	14 (All)
2.	I. Polavaram	11	11 (All)
3.	Mummidivaram	11	11 (All)
4.	P. Gannavaram	18	18 (All)
5.	Atreyapuram	15	15 (All)
6.	Ravulapalem	11	11 (All)
7.	Mamidikuduru	17	17 (All)
8.	Sakhinetipalli	8	8 (All)
9.	Malkipuram	11	11 (All)
10.	Kothapeta	10	10 (All)
11.	Razole	13	13 (All)
12.	Ambajipeta	13	13 (All)
13.	Allavaram	14	14 (All)
14.	Ainavilli	17	17 (All)
15.	Uppalaguptam	14	14 (All)
16.	Amalapuram	18	18 (All)

6th-7th November, 1996 Cyclone

A cyclone storm started in the Bay of Bengal on 5th November, 1996. It continued on a Westerly course on 6th November, 1996, dramatically picked up speed and moved in a West, North-Westerly direction and crossed the Andhra coast at about 10.30 p.m. on the intervening night of 6th/ 7th November, 1996. At the time of the landfall the wind speed recorded was of the order of 120 knots (221 kms/ Hour). Hence, the cyclone was of a very severe intensity.

Table 2.4: Particulars of Deaths and Ex gratia Paid during cyclone November, 96 in sample mandals of Amalapuram Revenue Division, E.G. Dt.

Sl. No.	Name of the Mandal	Deaths				Exgratia paid to eligible cases	
		Number of Reported	Number of identified	Un identified	Ineligible	Number	Amount paid (in Rs.)
1.	Katrenikona	230	80	150	—	80	80,00,000
2.	I. Polavaram	183	107	76	—	106	1,06,00,000
3.	Ainavilli	103	102	1	—	102	1,02,00,000
4.	Ambajipeta	76	62	14	—	62	62,00,000
5.	Amalapuram	43	40	3	—	40	40,00,000
Total		**635**	**391**	**244**	**—**	**390**	**3,90,00,000**

Table 2.5: Number of Missing cases and Ex-gratia paid during cyclone, November, 96 in sample mandals in Amalapuram Revenue Division, E.G. Dt.

Sl. No.	Name of the Mandal	Number of missing cases reported	Number of cases in which ex-gratia paid	Amount paid (Rs.)
1.	I. Polavaram	209	184	9,20,000
2.	Katrenikona	615	576	28,00,000
	Total	**824**	**760**	**37,20,000**

On the 6th day of November, 1996, at 5.30 p.m., it started with small drizzles and slowly got converted into rain with light winds. Within an hour, the rainfall pattern has increased and by 8.30 p.m., onwards there was sudden increase of rainfall with typical high velocity winds. The winds were possessing typical supersonic sounds, which were beyond human audibility or audio-decibels (the human audibility range is from 20 to 20,000 hertz) which means that it was not able to grasp or hear with human ear when big noisy sounds were created. The association of heavy rains with high velocity winds has resulted in

Table 2.6: Particulars of Injured cases & Remuneration paid to them due to cyclone, November, 96 in sample mandals in Amalapuram Revenue Division, E.G. District

Sl. No.	Name of the Mandal	Serious injuries received		Simple injuries received(Rs)	
		Number of cases	Amount paid (Rs)	Number of cases	Amount paid (Rs)
1.	Amalapuram	51	5,10,000	48	96,000
2.	Ainavilli	27	2,70,000	26	52,000
3.	Ambajipeta	45	4,50,000	89	1,78,000
4.	I. Polavaram	3	6,000	1	2,000
5.	Katrenikona	21	2,10,000	88	1,76,000
	Total	**147**	**14,46,000**	**252**	**5,04,000**

uprooting of trees (small to big), devastation and destruction of physical infrastructures such as buildings, houses, telephone and electric poles, blowing out of tiled and asbestos roofs, throwing out doors, window panes, tree branches from one place to another ranging from 200 mts to half k.m. distance. The examples are: Civil Supplies Godown in Amalapuram and the coconut trees. The entire devastation and damage had taken place within a gap of two and a half hours period, i.e., between 8.30 p.m. to 11.00 p.m. Several human deaths occurred in some places like Balusutippa and Bhyravapalem areas. The post cyclone

Table 2.7: Damages to Petty shops and Relief paid, during cyclone, Nov. 96 in Amalapuram Revenue Division, E.G. Dt.

Sl. No.	Name of the Mandal	Number of Petty shops damaged	Amount paid (Rs.)
1.	Amalapuram	2,764	27,64,000
2.	Ainavilli	756	7,56,000
3.	Ambajipeta	1,027	10,27,000
4.	I. Polavaram	739	7,22,000
5.	Katrenikona	810	81,000
	Total	**6,096**	**53,50,000**

Table 2.8: House damages and relief paid during the cyclone Nov. 96 Amalapuram Revenue Division, E.G. Dt.

Sl. No.	*Name of the Mandal*	*Number of Houses damaged*		*Amount paid for full damages*		*Amount paid for part damages*	
		Fully	*Partly*	*Monetary Relief*	*Additional Relief*	*Monetary Relief*	*Additional Relief*
1.	Amalapuram	20,643	7,851	2,06,43,000	41,28,600	39,25,500	—
2.	Ainavilli	11,521	5,984	1,15,21,000	23,04,200	29,92,000	14,96,800
3.	Ambajipeta	11,049	5,308	1,10,49,000	22,09,800	26,54,000	10,61,600
4.	I. Polavaram	20,616	685	2,06,16,000	41,23,200	3,42,500	—
5.	Katrenikona	21,019	754	2,10,19,000	42,03,800	3,77,000	—
	Total	**84,848**	**20,582**	**8,48,48,000**	**1,69,69,600**	**1,02,91,000**	**25,58,400**

Table 2.9: Cropped Area damaged in November, 96 cyclone in the sample mandals of Amalapuram Revenue Division, E.G. Dt.

Sl. No.	*Name of the Mandal*	*Total area fully damaged (Ha)*	*Area of S.F & MF fully damaged (Ha)*	*Number of SF & MF fully affected*	*Relief @ Rs. 625/Ha for SF & MF(Area x Rs.625)(Rs)*
1.	Amalapuram	3768	3436	8672	21,47,500
2.	Ainavilli	3943	2489	6939	15,55,625
3.	I. Polavaram	5070	3987	9396	24,91,875
4.	Katrenikona	5292	3843	7664	24,01,875
5.	Ambajipeta	1447	1068	3531	6,67,500
	Total	**19,520**	**14,823**	**36,202**	**92,64,375**

rain made the roads difficult even for pedestrians to walk. There were no communication and transporation facilities. The area was cut off from the main land and it led to total paralyse of normal human life.

--- Visual observation and feelings of
T. Baburao Naidu, the then Special Grade
Dy. Collector, Amalapuram.

Table 2.10: Damage to coconut plantations due to November, 96 cyclone in the sample mandals of Amalapuram Revenue Division, E.G. Dt.

Sl. No.	*Name of the Mandal*	*Coconut*			*Number of farmers involved*
		Extent involved in acres	*Number of trees Partial*	*Damaged Full*	
1.	Ambajipeta	8,413	3,08,696	2,19,213	14,486
2.	Ainavilli	7,541	3,05,214	3,00,048	15,739
3.	Katrenikona	6,583	2,69,025	2,79,722	14,147
4.	Amalapuram	6,522	3,40,872	2,73,711	20,739
5.	I. Polavaram	7,998	4,14,697	2,88,058	16,919
Total		**37,057**	**16,38,504**	**13,60,752**	**82,030**

Due to the severe cyclonic storm, which crossed the coast, South of Kakinada with gale winds of 120 knots, heavy damages were done to kacha/semi-permanent houses and crops resulting in huge losses of life and property, along with disruption of communication lines and electricity supply in almost all mandals in the District. The extent of damage in the selected mandals in terms of lives and property is presented in the following Tables, arrived at by the notification of Collector, East Godavari District.

Table 2.11: Particulars of Relief provided to affected fishermen for loss of Boats, Crafts, Tackles etc., during Cyclone, Nov. 96, in the sample mandals of Amalapuram Revenue Division, E.G.Dt.

Sl. No.	*Name of the Mandal*	*Number of beneficiaries*	*Relief amount distributed*
1.	Amalapuram	134	30,800
2.	Ainavilli	245	1,09,500
3.	Ambajipeta	86	46,700
4.	I. Polavaram	1,851	17,95,400
5.	Katrenikona	4,988	36,27,800
	Total	**7,304**	**56,10,200**

3

Profile of the Respondents

The present chapter deals exclusively with the socio-economic characteristics of the respondents. It is divided into two parts, with Part-A presenting the personal profile of the respondents, and Part-B presenting the household profile of the respondents.

Part-A

One of the basic objectives of this study is to examine the personal background of the respondents for understanding their attitudes on various related aspects like extent of damage, restoration and rehabilitation. The impact of cyclonic storm varies from person to person. A rich cyclone-affected farmer can get his original position within no time, whereas it is not the same case with a small farmer. The socio-economic status of the respondents determines the level of devastation and vis-à-vis their rehabilitation. The higher their socio-economic status, the quicker their process of rehabilitation and so on.

Personal Profile of the Sample Respondents

Data concerning religion, caste, sex composition, marital status, age structure, literacy level, occupation and income level of the respondents are presented in Table-3.1 to Table-3.8.

Religion: Religion shapes the attitudes and behaviours of the respondents. Hence, it has a significant bearing upon the study.

Table 3.1: Religion.

Mandal	*Hindu*	*Muslim*	*Christian*	*Total Respondents*
Amalapuram	85(100.0)	0(0.0)	0(0.0)	85(100.0)
Ambajipeta	66(84.6)	0(0.0)	12(15.4)	78(100.0)
I. Polavaram	131(100.0)	0(0.0)	0(0.0)	131(100.0)
Ainavilli	163(100.0)	0(0.0)	0(0.0)	163(100.0)
Katrenikona	142(99.3)	0(0.0)	1(0.7)	143(100.0)
Total	**587(97.8)**	**0(0.0)**	**13(2.2)**	**600(100.0)**

(Figures in parentheses indicate percentages)

Table-3.1 shows data pertaining to religion. Amalapuram, I.Polavaram and Ainavilli consist of cent per cent Hindu respondents. While Ambajipeta and Katrenikona consist of some Christian population along with the dominant Hindu religion and the sample has no Muslim population.

The overall scenario of religion reveals that 98 per cent of the sample belong to Hindu religion and 2 per cent belong to Christianity. The majority of Christian population are in Ambajipeta, with 15 per cent of 78 respondents, and they are converted scheduled caste population.

Caste: The caste system is one of the important elements of the Indian social structure. A social study or survey without the analysis of the caste structure, is erroneous. The traditional caste occupations are giving place to modern (caste-free) occupations. In the same way, the stigma attached to a particular occupation to a particular caste is waning away and other caste people are also taking the occupation without inhibitions, e.g. modern fish-processing Industry.

Table 3.2: Caste.

Mandal	*OC*	*BC*	*SC*	*ST*	*Total Respondents*
Amalapuram	34(40.0)	46(54.1)	5(5.9)	0(0.0)	85(100.0)
Ambajipeta	33(42.3)	12(15.4)	26(33.3)	7(9.0)	78(100.0)
I. polavaram	60(45.8)	54(41.2)	16(12.2)	1(0.8)	131(100.0)
Ainavilli	56(34.4)	42(25.8)	65(39.8)	0(0.0)	163(100.0)
Katrenikona	20(14.0)	72(50.3)	51(35.7)	0(0.0)	143(100.0)
Total	**203(33.8)**	**226(37.7)**	**163(27.2)**	**8(1.3)**	**600(100.0)**

(Figures in parentheses indicate percentages)

Table-3.2 shows data pertaining to the caste structure of the respondents. In Amalapuram mandal, out of 85 respondents, 40 per cent belong to forward castes, 54 per cent belong to Backward Castes and 6 per cent belong to Scheduled Castes. In Ambajipeta, out of 78 respondents, 42 per cent belong to Forward Castes, 15 per cent belong to Backward Castes, 33 per cent belong to Scheduled Castes and 9 per cent belong to Scheduled Tribes. I. Polavaram mandal consists of 131 respondents, and out of that, 46 per cent belong to Forward Castes, 41 per cent belong to Backward Castes, 12 per cent belong to Scheduled Castes and 0.8 per cent belong to Scheduled Tribes. In Ainavilli mandal, out of 163 respondents, 34 per cent belong to Forward Castes, 26 per cent belong to Backward Castes, and 40 per cent belong to Scheduled Castes. Katrenikona mandal consists of 143 respondents, out of that 14 per cent belong to Forward Castes, 50 per cent belong to Backward Castes, 36 per cent belong to Scheduled Castes.

The overall sample denotes that 34 per cent of the respondents belong to Forward Castes, 38 per cent belong to Backward Castes, 27 per cent belong to Scheduled Castes and a very small minority, i.e., 1.3 per cent belong to Scheduled Tribes. In Amalapuram and Katrenikona, Backward Castes respondents are more. In Ambajipeta, I. Polavaram and Ainavilli, there are of more Forward Castes respondents. Overall, the Scheduled Castes group comes under third position and the mandal-wise sample shows that Ambajipeta, Ainavilli and Katrenikona have more number of this group, compared to the other two. The sample consists of 9.8 per cent of Scheduled Tribes respondents, that too only, in two mandals, Ambajipeta and I. Polavaram, while the majority (9 per cent) are in Ambajipeta. On the whole, the data reveal that there is dominance of Backward Castes, besides, Forward Castes coming to the second largest group.

Sex Composition-Personal

The Indian society is a patriarchal society, wherein the head of the household is the male earning member. That is the reason for the emergence of majority of male respondents. In the case of female respondents, the majority are widows and 2 are unmarried. In the absence of the male head, the female or the wife is the next head of the household and in the absence or with the death of both parents, the eldest child is the respondent.

Table 3.3: Sex Composition-Personal.

Mandal	*Male*	*Female*	*Total Respondents*
Amalapuram	84(98.8)	1(1.2)	85(100.0)
Ambajipeta	73(93.6)	5(6.4)	78(100.0)
I. polavaram	126(96.2)	5(3.8)	131(100.0)
Ainavilli	157(96.3)	6(3.7)	163(100.0)
Katrenikona	131(91.6)	12(8.4)	143(100.0)
Total	**571(95.2)**	**29(4.8)**	**600(100.0)**

(Figures in parentheses indicate percentages)

Table-3.3. presents the data with regard to sex composition of the sample respondents. The data consist of 95 per cent male respondents and 5 per cent female respondents. The majority of female respondents are in Katrenikona mandal.

Marital Status: One of the important social aspects influencing the respondents alive is marital status with social responsibilities coming after marriage. So, to a certain extent, marital status effects their attitudes and opinions.

Table 3.4: Marital Status.

Mandal	*Married*	*Unmarried*	*Widow*	*Total Respondents*
Amalapuram	84(98.8)	0(0.0)	1(1.2)	85(100.0)
Ambajipeta	73(93.6)	1(1.3)	4(5.1)	78(100.0)
I. Polavaram	126(96.2)	0(0.0)	5(3.8)	131(100.0)
Ainavilli	156(95.7)	1(0.6)	6(3.7)	163(100.0)
Katrenikona	130(90.9)	2(1.4)	11(7.7)	143(100.0)
Total	**569(94.8)**	**4(0.7)**	**27(4.5)**	**600(100.0)**

(Figures in parentheses indicate percentages)

Table-3.4 presents the data with regard to the marital status of the respondents. The data show that 95 per cent of the sample are married. A small minority (4.5 per cent) of respondents are widows, with only one per cent being unmarried respondents. All the widows are female respondents and out of the four unmarried 2 are males and 2 are females. The data consist of 95 per cent of male married respondents, which is coterminus with the Indian family structure.

Age-Structure

Age is a key variable in understanding the socio-economic status of an individual. Sociologically, age denotes his/her status in a family, group or other organizational groups of society. Biologically, age has its significance as it denotes the physical and mental maturity of a person in the society. Keeping in view the relevance of age, data on the age structure of the sample respondents are discussed below:

Table 3.5: Age Structure.

Mandal	*20-29*	*30-39*	*40-49*	*50-59*	*60-69*	*70-79*	*Total Respondents*
Amalapuram	5 (5.9)	20 (23.5)	30 (35.3)	21 (24.7)	9 (10.6)	0 (0.0)	85 (100.0)
Ambajipeta	6 (7.7)	15 (19.2)	16 (20.5)	16 (20.5)	17 (21.8)	8 (10.3)	78 (100.0)
I. polavaram	6 (4.6)	53 (40.5)	37 (28.2)	22 (16.8)	11 (8.4)	2 (1.5)	131 (100.0)
Ainavilli	7 (4.3)	35 (21.5)	55 (33.7)	33 (20.2)	25 (15.3)	8 (5.0)	163 (100.0)
Katrenikona	20 (14.0)	32 (22.3)	42 (29.4)	21 (14.7)	23 (16.1)	5 (3.5)	143 (100.0)
Total	**44** **(7.3)**	**155** **(25.8)**	**180** **(30.0)**	**113** **(18.8)**	**85** **(14.2)**	**23** **(3.9)**	**600** **(100.0)**

(Figures in parentheses indicate percentages)
(X age = 46.31 years)

Table-3.5 shows data pertaining to the age structure of the respondents. In Amalapuram mandal, out of 85 respondents, 6 per cent belong to the age-group of 20-29, 24 per cent belong to the age-group of 30-39, 35 per cent belong to the age-group of 40-49, 25 per cent belong to the age-group of 50-59 and 11 per cent belong to the age-group of 60-69. In Amalapuram, the highest percentage of respondents (35) fall in the age group of 40-49.

In Ambajipeta mandal, out of 78 respondents from this mandal, 8 per cent belong to the age-group of 20-21, 19 per cent to the age-group of 30-31, 21 per cent each to the age-groups of 40-49 and 50-59, 22 per cent to the age-group of 60-69, 10 per cent to the age-group of 70-79. The above data show that there is significant percentage of (32) old respondents who belong to the age-groups of 60-69 and 70-79.

In I. Polavaram mandal, out of 131 respondents, 5 per cent belong to the age-group of 20-21, 41 per cent to the age-group of 30-39, 28 per cent to the age-group of 40-49,

17 per cent to the age-groups of 50-59, 8 per cent in the age-group of 60-69 and small proportion (1.5 per cent) to the age-group of 70-79. In this mandal, the highest percentage of respondents belong to the age group of 30-39.

In Ainavilli mandal, out of 163 respondents, 4 per cent are in the age-group of 20-29, 22 per cent are in the age-group of 30-39, 34 per cent in the age-group of 40-49, 20 per cent in the age-group of 50-59, 15 per cent in the age-group of 60-69 and 5 per cent in the age-group of 70-79.

In Katrenikona mandal, out of 143 respondents, 14 per cent are in the age-group of 20-29, 22 per cent in the age-group of 30-39, 29 per cent in the age-group of 40-49, 15 per cent in the age-group of 50-59, 16 per cent in the age-group of 60-69 and 4 per cent in the age-group of 70-79. The highest percentage of respondents in this mandal belong to the age-group of 40-49.

In the total sample of the 600 respondents, 7 per cent belong to the age-group of 20-29, 26 per cent belong to the age-group of 30-39, 30 per cent belong to the age group of 40-49, 19 per cent belong to the age-group of 50-59, 14 per cent to the age-group of 60-69, and 4 per cent to the age-group of 70-79. Thus, the sample respondents predominantly belong to the age-groups 30-39 40-49 (i.e., 56 per cent), who are mainly middle-aged. The percentage of the old respondents is 18.

All the five mandals predominantly have middle-aged respondents, who are in the age-groups of 30-39 and 40-49. The mean age of the respondents, which is 46.31 years also strengthens the above statement. Ambajipeta, Ainavilli and Katrenikona have more old respondents, in the age-groups of 60-69 and 70-79 than in Amalapuram and I. Polavaram.

Literacy Levels: The personality of individuals is developed by their literacy status. The respondents'

Table 3.6: Literacy Levels.

Mandal	*Illiterate*	*Primary*	*Upper Primary*	*Secondary*	*Inter*	*Degree*	*Others*	*Total Respondents*
Amalapuram	12(14.1)	25(29.4)	9(10.6)	13(15.3)	3(3.5)	16(18.8)	7(8.3)	85(100.0)
Ambajipeta	34(43.6)	14(17.9)	5(6.4)	12(15.4)	2(2.6)	10(12.8)	1(1.3)	78(100.0)
I. polavaram	74(56.5)	20(15.3)	16(12.2)	10(7.6)	4(3.1)	7(5.3)	0(0.0)	131(100.0)
Ainavilli	48(29.4)	62(38.0)	20(12.3)	19(11.7)	5(3.1)	6(3.7)	3(1.8)	163(100.0)
Katrenikona	116(81.1)	23(16.1)	1(0.7)	1(0.7)	2(1.4)	0(0.0)	0(0.0)	143(100.0)
Total	**284(47.3)**	**144(24.0)**	**51(8.5)**	**55(9.2)**	**16(2.7)**	**39(6.5)**	**11(1.8)**	**600(100.0)**

(Figures in parentheses indicate percentages)

attitudes and opinions show their maturity, which depends on the level of education. In the other way, it acts as a tool, in improving one's socio-economic status.

Table-3.6 presents the data pertaining to the literacy levels of the sample respondents. In Amalapuram, out of the 85 respondents, 14 per cent are illiterates, 29 per cent have studied up to primary, 11 per cent upto upper primary, 15 per cent upto secondary, 4 per cent upto Inter, 19 per cent upto Degree and 8 per cent belong to other category. The categories of others consist of highly and technically qualified persons. In Amalapuram, 27 per cent are highly qualified and it shows the educational forwardness of the region.

In Ambajipeta, out of 78 respondents, 44 per cent are illiterates, 18 per cent have studied upto primary, 6 per cent upto upper primary, 15 per cent upto secondary, 3 per cent upto Inter, 13 per cent upto Degree and one per cent are highly qualified.

In I. Polavaram, out of 131 respondents, 57 per cent are illiterates, (and 43 per cent are literates), 15 per cent studied upto primary, 12 per cent upto upper primary, 8 per cent upto secondary, and 8 per cent upto Degree and others.

In Ainavilli mandal, out of 163 respondents, 29 per cent are illiterates, 38 per cent studied upto primary level, 12 per cent each upto Upper Primary and Secondary levels, 3 per cent upto Inter, and 5 per cent upto Degree and other levels. Overall, the literate population is 71 percent.

In Katrenikona, out of 143 respondents, majority are (81 per cent) are illiterates, 16 per cent with primary level, less than one per cent each with Upper Primary and Secondary levels and one per cent with Inter. The data show the educational backwardness of the area.

The overall scenario shows that 47 per cent are illiterates and 53 per cent are literates. Out of the total,

Table 3.7: Occupation Structure.

Mandal	*Agriculture*	*Coconut Plantation*	*Private Job*	*Govt. Service*	*Weaving*	*Self-Employment*	*Fishing*	*Service*	*Agricultural Labour*	*Total Respondents*
Amalapuram	7(8.2)	11(12.9)	3(3.5)	17(20.0)	24(28.2)	4(4.7)	0(0.0)	10(11.8)	9(10.7)	85(100.0)
Ambajipeta	5(6.4)	17(21.8)	2(2.6)	10(12.8)	1(1.3)	0(0.0)	0(0.0)	5(6.4)	38(48.7)	78(100.0)
I. Polavaram	45(34.4)	10(7.6)	1(0.8)	4(3.1)	0(0.0)	8(6.1)	40(30.5)	2(1.5)	21(16.0)	131(100.0)
Ainavilli	54(33.1)	23(14.1)	1(0.6)	3(1.8)	1(0.6)	6(3.6)	3(1.8)	5(3.2)	67(41.2)	163(100.0)
Katrenikona	56(39.2)	4(2.8)	0(0.0)	1(0.7)	0(0.0)	2(1.4)	48(33.6)	3(2.1)	29(20.2)	143(100.0)
Total	**167(27.8)**	**65(10.8)**	**7(1.2)**	**35(5.8)**	**26(4.3)**	**20(3.3)**	**91(15.3)**	**25(4.2)**	**164(27.3)**	**600(100.0)**

(Figures in parentheses indicate percentages)

24 per cent studied upto Primary, 9 per cent each upto Upper Primary and Secondary, 3 per cent upto Inter and 8 per cent are highly and technically qualified and as such, are with a better edge, compared to other mandals with regard to literacy.

Occupation Structure: Occupation is one of the important factors in the determination of an individual's socio-economic status. India is a land of villages and majority of Indian people depend on agriculture and related activities. Even this study corroborates with the above fact.

Table-3.7 presents the data with regard to occupation structure of the sample respondents. Out of 85 respondents in Amalapuram mandal, 8 per cent are engaged in agriculture, 13 per cent are in coconut plantation, 4 per cent are in private jobs, 20 per cent are weavers, 5 per cent are self-employed, 12 per cent are engaged in service occupations like barbers, tailors etc., and 11 per cent are agricultural labourers. The highest percentage of respondents in Amalapuram (one of the sample villages in Amalapuram, i.e., Bandarulanka, is particularly a weavers' village), is engaged in weaving (28 per cent) and Government Service (20 per cent). The landholding families are 21 per cent and 11 per cent are agricultural labourers.

In Ambajipeta, out of 78 respondents, 6 per cent are engaged in Agriculture, 22 per cent are in coconut platations, (28 per cent are landholding families), 3 per cent are doing private jobs, 13 per cent are working in Government services, 1 per cent are weavers, 6 per cent are doing service occupations and, significantly the highest percentage (49 per cent) of the sample are agricultural labourers.

In I. Polavaram, out of 131 respondents, the land-holding families (34 per cent in Agriculture + 8 per cent in coconut plantations) consist of 42 per cent, less than one per cent are in private jobs, 3 per cent are in Government services, 6 per cent are in self-employment, 31 per cent are engaged in fishing, 2 per cent are engaged in service occupations and 16 per cent are agricultural labourers. Agriculture and fishing are the dominant occupations in this mandal, with G. Moolapalem being a fishing village.

In Ainavilli mandal, out of 163 respondents, the land-holding families consist of 47 per cent (with 33 per cent in agriculture + 14 in coconut plantation), less than one per cent engaged in private jobs, 2 per cent in Government services, less than one percent are in weaving, 4 percent in self-employment, 2 per cent in fishing, 3 per cent doing service occupations and 41 per cent working as agricultural labourers.

In Katrenikona, out of 143 respondents, 42 per cent are landholders (39 per cent in agriculture + 3 per cent in coconut plantation), less than one per cent are in Government services, 1 per cent in self-employment, 34 per cent engaged in fishing, 2 per cent in service occupations and 20 per cent are agricultural labourers.

The overall occupational scenario shows that the sample consists of 39 per cent of landholders in agriculture (28 per cent in agriculture + 11 per cent in coconut plantation), 1 per cent of private jobholders, 6 per cent of Government job-holders, 4 per cent of weavers, 3 per cent of self-employed, 15 per cent of fishermen, 4 per cent are barbers, tailors, carpenters, purohits, electricians, masons etc., and 27 per cent are agricultural labourers. The data reveal that agriculture is the dominant occupation (39 per cent) and respondents who are engaged in this field are comparatively on a better edge than others. Next are agricultural labourers, with the highest percentage (27). Fishing is another major occupation with 15 per cent. On the whole, agriculture and fishing are the major occupations in this region.

Income Levels:-In the modern society, income is one of the most important bases of social differentiation and of distribution of power, prestige and privilege in the society, besides caste.

Table-3.8 presents data with regard to income levels of the respondents. In Amalapuram, out of 85 respondents, one per cent belong to less than Rs. 5000 category, a majority (73 per cent) belong to Rs. 5000-15000 category, one per cent belong to Rs. 15000-25000 category, 7 per cent belong to Rs.25000-35000 category, one per cent each belong to Rs.35000-45000 and Rs.45000-55000 categories, and, significantly, 15 per cent belong to the highest income level, i.e., Rs.55000-65000 category.

In Ambajipeta, out of 78 respondents, one per cent belong to less than Rs.5000 category, 77 per cent belong to Rs.5000-15000 category, which forms a majority, one per cent belong to Rs.15000-25000, 4 per cent belong to Rs.25000-35000, there are no respondents in the categories of Rs.35000-45000 and Rs.45000-55000 and 17 per cent belong to the highest category, i.e., Rs.55000-65000.

In I. Polavaram, out of 131 respondents, 20 per cent belong to less than Rs. 5000 category, 36 per cent belong to Rs.5000-15000 category, 18 per cent belong to Rs.15000 - 25000 category, 12 per cent belong to Rs.25000-35000 category, 8 per cent belong to Rs. 35000-45000 category, 5 per cent belong to Rs. 45000-55000 category and only 3 per cent belong to the highest category, i.e., Rs.55000-65000.

In Ainavilli mandal, out of 163 respondents, 18 per cent are in the category of <5000, 66 per cent are in the category of Rs.5000-15000, 7 per cent are in the category of Rs.15000-25000, 3 per cent each are in the categories of Rs.25000-35000 Rs.35000-45000, and Rs.45000-55000 and even less than one per cent are in the highest category, i.e., Rs.55000-65000.

In Katrenikona mandal, out of 143 respondents, significantly, 41 per cent belong to less than Rs.5000

Table 3.8: Income levels.

Mandal	*<5000*	*5000-15000*	*15000-25000*	*25000-35000*	*35000-45000*	*45000-55000*	*55000-65000*	*Total Respondents*
Amalapuram	1(1.2)	62(72.9)	1(1.2)	6(7.2)	1(1.2)	1(1.2)	13(15.3)	85(100.0)
Ambajipeta	1(1.3)	60(76.9)	1(1.3)	3(3.8)	0(0.0)	0(0.0)	13(16.7)	78(100.0)
I. Polavaram	26(19.8)	47(35.9)	23(17.6)	15(11.5)	10(7.6)	6(4.6)	4(3.0)	131(100.0)
Ainavilli	29(17.8)	108(66.3)	11(6.7)	5(3.0)	5(3.0)	4(2.6)	1(0.6)	163(100.0)
Katrenikona	59(41.0)	83(58.0)	0(0.0)	0(0.0)	1(1.0)	0(0.0)	0(0.0)	143(100.0)
Total	**116(19.3)**	**360(60.0)**	**36(6.0)**	**29(4.8)**	**17(2.8)**	**11(1.8)**	**31(5.3)**	**600(100.0)**

(Figures in parentheses indicate percentages)
(X income = Rs.14,283.3)

category and 58 per cent belong to Rs.5000-15000 category and there are no respondents in other higher categories, except one per cent in Rs.35000-45000 category. This shows the poor economic scenario of respondents in Katrenikona.

The overall income levels of the respondents show that out of 600 respondents, 19 per cent are in the lowest category, the majority (60 per cent) are in the category of Rs.5000-15000, 6 per cent are in the category of Rs.15000 -25000, 5 per cent are in the Rs.25000 -35000 category, 3 per cent are in the Rs.35000-45000 category, 2 per cent are in the category of Rs.45000-55000 and only 5 per cent are in the highest group who are having Rs.55000-65000 per annum. The majority of respondents happen to fall in the category of Rs.5000-15000 and mean income level is Rs.14,283.3. The above data show that there is a lot of variation in the income levels of the respondents and the high income group (Rs.45000-65000) is only 7 per cent, which shows the poor economic scenario of the sample respondents.

Part-B

Household Particulars of the Sample Respondents

Type of Family

Table-3.9 presents data with regard to the type of family.

Total 3.9: Type of Family.

Mandal	*Joint*	*Nuclear*	*Extended*	*Total Respondents*
Amalapuram	0(0.0)	85(100.0)	0(0.0)	85(100.0)
Ambajipeta	0(0.0)	77(98.7)	1(1.3)	78(100.0)
I. polavaram	0(0.0)	131(100.0)	0(0.0)	131(100.0)
Ainavilli	1(0.6)	155(95.1)	7(4.3)	163(100.0)
Katrenikona	0(0.0)	143(100.0)	0(0.0)	143(100.0)
Total:	**1(0.2)**	**591(98.5)**	**8(1.3)**	**600(100.0)**

(Figures in parentheses indicate percentages)

The family status is considered as the basic element of social organization. Irrespective of rural or urban background, the type of family in which respondents live makes a difference in their attitude towards their living and other life styles and life chances.

In Amalapuram, I.Polavaram, and Katrenikona, all the sample respondents are living in nuclear families, whereas in Ambajipeta, majority (98.7 per cent) are living in nuclear and only one household is in extended family. In Ainavilli mandal, one family is joint family, 4.3 per cent are living in extended families and the majority (95 per cent) are having nuclear families.

The total sample reveals that majority (98.5) per cent are having nuclear type of families, and 1.3 per cent are having extended families. Only one joint family exists in the total sample and this shows the changing trend with regard to the type of family.

Size of the Household

The size of the household is another important characteristic of the family in the changing structure of the family. A household may consist of one person or more than one. But, the nuclear family minimises its size of the household, due to the changing needs of the society.

Table 3.10: Size of House hold.

Mandal	*1-2*	*3-4*	*5-6*	*>7*	*T*
Amalapuram	17(19.8)	22(26.2)	46(54.0)	0(0.0)	85(100.0)
Ambajipeta	38(48.6)	22(28.6)	18(22.8)	0(0.0)	78(100.0)
I. Polavaram	30(23.1)	71(53.5)	7(5.4)	23(18.0)	131(100.0)
Ainavilli	66(39.6)	60(37.1)	21(13.0)	16(10.3)	163(100.0)
Katrenikona	20(14.3)	49(34.0)	21(15.0)	53(36.7)	143(100.0)
Total	**171(29.0)**	**224(37.3)**	**113(18.7)**	**92(15.0)**	**600(100.0)**

(Figures in parentheses indicate percentages)
(X size = 3.9 members)

Table-3.10 presents the data with regard to the size of the household of the respondents. In Amalapuram, the total size is 85, out of that, 20 per cent are having 1-2 members, 26 per cent are with 3-4 members, the highest percentage (54) falls with 5-6 members and there is no household with more than 7 members.

In Ambajipeta, the total size is 78 members and out of that 49 percent are having 1-2 members, 29 percent are with 3-4 members, 23 percent are with 5-6 and there is no household with more than 7 members.

In I. Polavaram, the total size is 131. Out of that, 23 per cent are having 1-2 members, the majority (54 per cent) are having 3-4 members, 5 per cent are with 5-6 members and 18 per cent (G.Moolapalem having the highest size with 80 members and it happened to be a fishing village) having more than 7 family members.

In Ainavilli, the total size is 163. Out of that, 40 per cent are with 1-2 members, 37 per cent are with 3-4 members, 13 per cent are with 5-6 members and 10 per cent are having more than 7 family members in their household (Pottilanka is a fishing village).

In Katrenikona, the total size is 143. Out of that, 14 per cent are with 1-2 members, 34 per cent are with 3-4 members, 15 per cent are with 5-6 and, significantly, 37 per cent are having more than 7 members. Fishing villages are more in this mandal.

The total number of members in the household as for the 600 respondents shows that 29 per cent are having 1-2 members (which shows the small size of the household with increasing nuclear setups and increasing popularity of family planning programmes), 37 per cent are having 3-4 members, 19 per cent are with 5-6 members and 15 per cent are with more than 7 members. The above data reveal that the mandals like I. Polavaram, Ainavilli and

Katrenikona, which are having fishing villages, show the highest size of the household. This reveals that there is no impact of family planning programmes with the fishermen community because of high illiteracy, ignorance and above all even a small child in this community is a helping hand to their parents. A 5-year old boy also goes for fishing or a girl engages in prawn-seed-catching and the parents won't feel that the children are burden to them. Even the old-men, who cannot go for fishing will be engaged in doing nets and other such fishing activities. On the whole, the highest percentage (38) fall with 3-4 size of the household which is equivalent to Indian average size of the household, and the mean size of the household (3.9) also substantiates the above statement.

Sex Composition of the Household

Table-3.11 presents data with regard to sex composition of members of the household.

Table 3.11: Sex Composition-House Hold.

Mandal	*Male*	*Female*	*Child*			*Total*
			Male	*Female*	*Total*	*Respondents*
Amalapuram	136(47.4)	133(46.3)	11(3.9)	7(2.4)	18(6.3)	287(100.0)
Ambajipeta	122(46.4)	128(48.7)	9(3.4)	4(1.5)	13(4.9)	263(100.0)
I. Polavaram	293(50.9)	247(42.8)	24(4.2)	12(2.1)	36(6.3)	576(100.0)
Ainavilli	363(51.1)	293(41.3)	33(4.6)	21(3.0)	54(7.6)	710(100.0)
Katrenikona	341(53.8)	216(34.1)	49(7.7)	28(4.4)	77(12.1)	634(100.0)
Total	**1255(50.8)**	**1017(41.2)**	**126(5.1)**	**72(2.9)**	**198(8.0)**	**2470(100.0)**

(Figures in parentheses indicate percentages)

In Amalapuram mandal, out of 287, 47 per cent happen to be males, 46 per cent happen to be females and 6 per cent happen to be children. In Ambajipeta, out of 263, 46 per cent happen to be males, 49 per cent happen to be females and 5 per cent are children. In I. Polavaram, out of 576, 51 percent are males, 43 per cent are females and 6 per cent are children. In Ainavilli mandal, out of 710, 51 per cent are males, 41 per cent are females and 8 per cent are children. In Katrenikona, out of 634, 54 per cent are males, 34 per cent are females and 12 per cent are children. Out of the total 2,470 members, 2,282 are adults and 198 are children.

The data show that, among the adults, there is 51 per cent males, 41 per cent females and 8 per cent children. The sex ratio is favourable to males.

Total Earning Members

Table-3.12 presents the data with regard to the total number of economically active members in a household. The more the active members, the more the financial capability of the household and vice versa.

Total 3.12: Total Earning Members.

Mandal	*1*	*2-3*	*4-5*	*6+*	*Total Respondents*
Amalapuram	37(43.5)	46(54.1)	1(1.2)	1(1.2)	85(100.0)
Ambajipeta	32(41.0)	44(56.4)	2(2.6)	0(0.0)	78(100.0)
I. Polavaram	33(25.2)	92(70.2)	6(7.6)	0(0.0)	131(100.0)
Ainavilli	64(39.2)	73(44.8)	26(16.0)	0(0.0)	163(100.0)
Katrenikona	48(33.6)	57(39.9)	29(20.3)	9(6.2)	143(100.0)
Total	**214(35.7)**	**312(52.0)**	**64(10.7)**	**10(1.6)**	**600(100.0)**

(Figures in parentheses indicate percentages)
(X earners = 2.1)

In Amalapuram mandal, out of 85 households, 44 per cent of the households belong to single earning category, 54 per cent are in the category of 2-3 earning members and one per cent each in the categories of 4-5 and 6 + categories.

In Ambajipeta, out of 78 households, 41 per cent of the households are having single earners, 56 per cent with 2-3 earners, 3 per cent with 4-5 earners. In I. Polavaram, one-quarter of the total of 131 households is having one earner, majority (70 per cent) are with 2-3 earners and 8 per cent with 4-5 earning members.

In Ainavilli mandal, out of 163 households, 39 per cent belong to single earning member category, 45 per cent belong to 2-3 earning members, and 16 per cent are in 4-5 category. In Katrenikona, out of 143 households, one-third of the households are in single earning member category, 40 per cent are with 2-3 earning members, 20 per cent are with 4-5 earning members and six per cent households are with more than 6 earning members.

Out of the total 600 households, 36 per cent households are having only one respondent as the earning member, 52 per cent are having 2-3 earning members, 11 per cent are having 4-5 earning members and 2 per cent are with more than six earning members. On the whole, Amalapuram (44 per cent) has the more single earner households, I. Polavaram (with 70 per cent) has the more 2-3 earner households and Katrenikona has the more multiple earning members (4-6+). In fishing communities, even a small child goes for fishing and the result is more number of earning members. The data reveal that majority (52 per cent) of the households are having 2-3 earning members and the mean size of the earning members is 2:1.

Literacy Levels of the Household

Table-3.13 presents the data with regard to the literacy levels of the household members. In Amalapuram, out of 287 members, 15 per cent are illiterate, 28 per cent studied upto primary, 12 per cent studied upto upper primary, 19 per cent upto secondary, 11 percent upto Inter, 13 per cent upto Degree and only 4 per cent studied post-graduation and other technical courses. That means, 17 per cent of the household members are highly qualified.

In Ambajipeta, out of 263 members, 34 per cent are illiterate, 22 per cent studied upto primary, 9 per cent upto

Table 3.13: Literacy Levels of the Households.

Mandal	*Illiterate*	*Primary*	*Upper Primary*	*Secondary*	*Inter*	*Degree*	*Others*	*Total Respondents*
Amalapuram	43(15.0)	79(27.5)	33(11.5)	53(18.5)	31(10.8)	37(12.9)	11(3.8)	287(100.0)
Ambajipeta	88(33.5)	58(22.1)	24(9.1)	44(16.7)	17(6.5)	29(11.0)	3(1.1)	263(100.0)
I. Polavaram	257(44.6)	108(18.6)	84(14.7)	59(10.3)	45(7.8)	16(2.8)	7(1.2)	576(100.0)
Ainavilli	136(19.2)	203(28.6)	119(16.8)	120(16.9)	71(10.0)	45(6.2)	16(2.3)	710(100.0)
Katrenikona	491(77.4)	87(13.7)	28(4.4)	19(3.1)	6(0.9)	3(0.5)	0(0.0)	634(100.0)
Total	**1015(41.0)**	**535(21.7)**	**288(11.7)**	**295(11.9)**	**170(6.9)**	**130(5.3)**	**37(1.5)**	**2470(100.0)**

(Figures in parentheses indicate percentages)

upper primary, 17 per cent upto secondary, 7 per cent upto Inter and 12 per cent studied upto Degree and other courses.

In I. Polavaram mandal, out of 576 members, the majority are illiterate (45 per cent), 19 per cent studied upto primary, 15 per cent upto Upper primary, 10 per cent upto Secondary, 8 per cent upto Inter and only 4 per cent studied upto Degree and other courses.

In Ainavilli mandal, out of 710 members, 19 per cent are illiterates, 29 per cent studied upto Primary, 17 per cent each upto Upper primary and Secondary, 10 per cent upto Inter and 8 per cent upto Degree and other courses.

In Katrenikona, a little more than three-fourths of the members are illiterate. Out of 634 members, 14 per cent studied upto primary, 4 per cent upto upper primary, 3 per cent upto Secondary, less than one percent upto Inter and only 0.5 per cent have higher levels of literacy.

On the whole, out of 2,470 members, 41 per cent are illiterate, 22 per cent studied upto Primary, 12 per cent each upto Upper Primary and Secondary, 7 per cent upto Inter and significantly less number (6.5 per cent) have high literacy levels, which shows the poor literacy background.

The data reveal that Katrenikona mandal has the most illiterate population (77 per cent); Amalapuram and Ambajipeta are having relatively highly literate population (16 per cent and 12 per cent) respectively. On the whole, the data reveal that more than one-third of the household members are illiterate and one-fifth of the household members studied upto primary level only. Comparatively, Amalapuram, Ambajipeta and Ainavilli mandals are better than other mandals in terms of literacy levels.

Occupational Structure of Other Members of the Household

Table-3.14 presents the data with regard to the occupational structure of the respondent households. The

Total 3.14: Occupational Structure of Households.

Mandal	*Agri-culture*	*Coconut Plantation*	*Private Job*	*Govt. Service*	*Weaving*	*Self-Employ-ment*	*Fishing*	*Service*	*Agricultural Labour*	*Not Relevant*	*Total Respondents*
Amalapuram	9(3.2)	11(3.8)	3(1.0)	20(6.9)	55(19.2)	5(1.8)	0(0.0)	14(4.9)	21(7.3)	149(51.9)	287(100.0)
Ambajipeta	13(4.9)	17(6.5)	3(1.1)	16(6.1)	1(0.4)	0(0.0)	0(0.0)	7(2.7)	72(27.4)	134(50.9)	263(100.0)
I. Polavaram	54(9.4)	10(1.7)	2(0.3)	4(0.8)	0(0.0)	8(1.4)	158(27.4)	6(1.0)	47(8.2)	287(49.8)	576(100.0)
Ainavilli	93(13.1)	23(3.2)	7(1.1)	3(0.4)	2(0.3)	16(2.3)	17(2.4)	13(1.8)	224(31.5)	312(43.8)	710(100.0)
Katrenikona	152(24.0)	4(0.6)	2(0.3)	1(0.2)	0(0.0)	4(0.6)	209(33.0)	6(0.9)	109(17.2)	147(23.2)	634(100.0)
Total	**321(13.1)**	**65(2.6)**	**17(0.7)**	**44(1.8)**	**58(2.3)**	**33(1.3)**	**384(15.5)**	**46(1.9)**	**473(19.1)**	**1029(41.7)**	**2470(100.0)**

(Figures in parentheses indicate percentages)

total size of the households is 2,470. Out of that 1,029 (42 per cent) are non-working members and 1,441 (58 percent) are economically active members.

In Amalapuram mandal, out of 287 members, 3 per cent are engaged in agriculture, 4 percent are engaged in coconut plantation, one per cent are in private service, 7 per cent are in Government service, 19 per cent are in weaving, 20 per cent are in self-employment, 5 per cent are in service occupations, 7 per cent are agricultural labourers and significantly, a little more than half (52 per cent) are non-working members.

In Ambajipeta, out of 263 members, 5 per cent are engaged in agriculture, 7 per cent are in coconut plantations, one per cent are in private jobs, 6 per cent are in Government jobs, 0.4 per cent are weavers, 3 per cent are in service occupations, 27 per cent are agricultural labourers and 51 per cent are non-working members.

In I. Polavaram, out of 576 members, 9 per cent are engaged in agriculture, 2 per cent are in coconut plantation, 1.2 per cent in private and Government jobs, 27 per cent in fishing, one per cent in service occupations, 8 per cent working as agricultural labourers and 50 per cent are non-working members.

In Ainavilli mandal, out of 710 members, 13 per cent are engaged in agriculture, 3 per cent are in coconut plantation, 1.5 per cent are in Private and Government jobs, 0.3 per cent are in weaving, 2 per cent each are in self-employment, fishing and service occupations. Significantly 32 per cent are engaged as agricultural labourers and 44 per cent are non-working members.

In Katrenikona mandal, out of 634 members, significantly, 24 per cent are engaged in agriculture, 0.6 per cent in coconut plantation, 0.5 per cent each are in Private and Government sector, 0.6 per cent in self-employment, one-third in fishing, 0.9 per cent in service occupations, 17 per cent working as agricultural labourers and very interestingly only 23 per cent are non-working members.

Out of the 2,470 of total households, 13 per cent are engaged in agriculture, 3 per cent are engaged in coconut plantation, 2.5 per cent are in Private jobs and Government jobs, 2.3 per cent are in weaving, 1.3 per cent are in self-employment, 16 per cent are in fishing, 2.0 per cent are in service occupations, 19 per cent are agricultural labourers and, significantly (42 per cent) are non-working members.

The comparisons of mandals show that in Katrenikona more number (25 per cent) of members are engaged in agriculture compared to other mandals. In I. Polavaram and Katrenikona more members are engaged in fishing in Ainavilli (39 per cent) the highest number are agricultural labourers. Significantly, less number are non-working members in Katrenikona compared to other mandals.

On the whole, occupations like agricultural labourers, fishing and agriculture come in first, second and third positions. Overall, 42 per cent are non-active members and 58 per cent are active in terms of occupation.

Total Family Income

Table-3.15 presents the data with regard to total family income including the respondent's income.

In Amalapuram, out of 85 respondents, one per cent are in less than Rs.5000 category, 38 per cent belong to Rs.5000-15000 category, 29 per cent are in Rs.15000-25000, 8 per cent belong to Rs.25000-35000 category, 5 per cent are in Rs.35000-45000 category, one per cent are in Rs.45000-55000 category and 18 per cent are in the highest category, i.e., Rs.55000-65000. That means, in Amalapuram mandal, 19 per cent are in the income levels of (Rs.45,000-65000) with high income level, 42 per cent are with middle income level (Rs.15,000-45,000) and 39 per cent are with low income level (Rs.<5,000-15,000).

Total 3.15: Total Household Income.

Mandal	*<5000*	*5000-15000*	*15000-25000*	*25000-35000*	*35000-45000*	*45000-55000*	*55000-65000*	*Total Respondents*
Amalapuram	1(1.2)	32(37.6)	25(29.4)	7(8.2)	4(4.7)	1(1.3)	15(17.6)	85(100.0)
Ambajipeta	0(0.0)	50(64.2)	9(11.5)	3(3.8)	0(0.0)	0(0.0)	16(20.5)	78(100.0)
I. Polavaram	14(10.6)	50(38.3)	28(21.4)	19(14.5)	10(7.6)	5(3.8)	5(3.8)	131(100.0)
Ainavilli	5(3.2)	112(68.7)	27(16.6)	9(5.5)	4(2.5)	4(2.5)	2(1.0)	163(100.0)
Katrenikona	35(24.4)	95(66.4)	9(6.3)	3(2.2)	1(0.7)	0(0.0)	0(0.0)	143(100.0)
Total	**55(9.2)**	**339(56.5)**	**98(16.3)**	**41(6.8)**	**19(3.2)**	**10(1.7)**	**38(6.3)**	**600(100.0)**

(Figures in parentheses indicate percentages)
(X Household Income = Rs.17,095.8)

Amalapuram Total Household Income			Amalapuram Individual Respondent's Income
High	-	19 per cent	16 per cent
Middle	-	42 per cent	10 per cent
Low	-	39 per cent	74 per cent

The above figures show that with the total family income, the respondents climbed up in the economic ladder. There is much increase from low to middle and 3 per cent increase from middle to high. Finally, we can say that majority of the respondents fall in middle income category in Amalapuram.

In Ambajipeta, out of 78 respondents, 64 per cent fall in the category of less than Rs.5000-15000, 12 per cent belong to Rs.15000-25000, 4 per cent to Rs.25000-35000 income and 20 per cent belong to the highest category, i.e., Rs.55000-65000.

Total household Income			Respondent's Income
High	-	20 per cent	17 per cent
Middle	-	16 per cent	5 per cent
Low	-	64 per cent	78 per cent

It means majority of the respondents in Ambajipeta belong to low income category. There is no drastic increase from low to middle while 4 per cent increase is there from middle to high income group.

In I. Polavaram, out of 131 respondents, 10.6 per cent belong to less than Rs.5000 category, 38 per cent belong to Rs.5000-15000, 21 per cent to Rs.15000-25000, 15 per cent to Rs.25000-35000, 8 per cent to Rs.35000-45000 and 4 per cent each to Rs.45000-55000 and Rs.55000-65000 income category.

Total household Income			Respondent's Income
High	-	8 per cent	8 per cent
Middle	-	43 per cent	36 per cent
Low	-	49 per cent	56 per cent

The above figures show that nearly half of the respondents are in low income group. There is 7 per cent increase from low to middle and there is no change from middle to high income group.

In Ainavilli mandal, out of 163 respondents, 3 per cent belong to less than Rs.5000 category, 68 per cent belong to Rs.5000-15000 category, 17 per cent are in Rs.15000-25000, 6 per cent are in Rs.25000-35000, 2.5 per cent each in the category of Rs.35000-45000 and Rs.45000-55000 and one per cent are in the highest category of Rs.55000-65000.

Total household Income			Respondent's Income
High	-	3per cent	3 per cent
Middle	-	26 per cent	13 per cent
Low	-	72 per cent	84 per cent

The above figures reveal that the majority of the respondents belong to low income group. There is 12 per cent increase from low to middle and there is no change from middle to high.

In Katrenikona mandal, out of 143 respondents, 24 per cent belong to less than Rs.5000 category, 66 per cent are in Rs.5000-15000, 6 per cent are in Rs.15000-25000, 2 per cent are in Rs.25000-35000, 0.7 per cent are in the Rs.35000-45000 category and there are no respondents in the high income group.

Total household Income			Respondent's Income
High	-	0 per cent	0 per cent
Middle	-	9 per cent	1 per cent
Low	-	91 per cent	99 per cent

The above data reveals that the Katrenikona mandal is economically very backward. Significantly 91 per cent of households belong to low income group. Interestingly, 26 per cent of the households in Katrenikona have more than 4 earning members, but it happened to be that their earnings are very meager.

The overall data with regard to total household income project that 9 per cent are in less than Rs.5000 category, 51 per cent are in Rs.5000-15000 category, 16 per cent are in Rs.15000-25000 category, 7 per cent belong to Rs.25000-35000, 3 per cent are in Rs.35000-45000, 2 per cent are in Rs.45000-55000 and only 6 per cent belong to the highest income category, i.e., Rs.55000-65000.

Total overall household Income			Respondent's Income
High	-	8per cent	7 per cent
Middle	-	26 per cent	14 per cent
Low	-	66 per cent	79 per cent

The above data show that majority of the respondents belong to low income households. There is 12 per cent increase from low to middle and one per cent increase from middle to high with regard to respondents' income, while taking into his/her household income into consideration.

Comparatively, Amalapuram and I. Polavaram are financially better off than their other counterpart mandals in the sample. Interestingly, in Ambajipeta, high income households are more than middle income even though the mandal consists of more low income families.

Looking at the overall data on the socio-economic structure of the respondents, the following conclusions can be made. The socio-economic data of the respondents indicate there is predominance of Hindu religion. The caste structure of the respondents denotes that 38 per cent of the respondents belong to Backward Castes followed by Forward Castes with 34 per cent Scheduled Caste with 27 per cent and a small minority of Scheduled Tribes. The sample consists of 95 per cent of male respondents and 5 per cent of female respondents. The reason for the predominance of male respondents is that of a patriarchal nature of society wherein usually the head of the household is a male member. The data consist of 95 per cent male married respondents which is coterminous with the Indian family structure mostly patrilineal. Majority (56 per cent) of the respondents are in their middle age (30-49). The mean age of the respondents is 46.3. The literacy levels of the respondents show that a little less than half are significantly illiterate, one-fourth of the respondents have studied upto primary level and only 8 per cent of the total sample have good academic background. The occupational structure of the respondents reveals that in Konaseema, the sample consists of 39 per cent landholders. Significantly, a little more than one-fourth are agricultural labourers. It shows that 66 per cent of the respondents are dependent on agriculture and the devastating impact of cyclone varies from cultivator to agricultural labourer. Next, fishing is another major occupation of the respondents. The income levels of the respondents show that nearly 80 per cent are with low income, and only 7 per cent belong to the highest income groups. The mean size of the income of the respondents is Rs.14,283.3.

The household particulars of the respondents reveal that majority are living in nuclear families with three to four family members. The mean size of the household is 3.9 members. The sex composition of the household is favourable to male members. Half of the households have 2-3 earning members. The mean size of the earning members is 2.1. The literacy levels of the household shows that significant number are illiterate (41 per cent). The occupational structure of the household is the same to that of the respondents with predominance of agriculture and fishing as occupations. The economic scenario shows that majority of the households belong to low income groups. The mean size of the total household income is Rs.17,095.8.

4

Damage Assessment

As is already seen the severe cyclonic storm which crossed the East Coast, South of Kakinada town, with gale winds of 120 knots, struck in its wake, heavy damages to crops, coconut plantations and houses resulting in huge losses to life and property along with disruption of communication lines and electricity supply in almost all mandals in East Godavari District. Earlier in this study in the Introductory chapter, damage assessment is presented based on the Revenue Divisions of East Godavari District. The devastation data of the selected mandals from Amalapuram Revenue Division are given in the profile of the Study Area. Presently, in this chapter, the extent of damage in the selected mandals is being described and analysed using the primary data and keeping in view the overall devastation scenario of the District using the East Godavari District Collector's notification.

The chapter is divided into Three Parts. Part-A presents the extent of damage to lives and property while Part-B explains the restoration struggle of the respondents with Part-C culls out rescue operations taking into consideration the adequacy of Rehabilitation facilities as can be known from the opinions of the respondents.

Part-A

Damage to Lives

In East Godavari District, as per the Damage

Assessment Committee's indications and police F.I.Rs, there were 978 cases reported as dead out of which 666 cases are identified, 296 cases being unidentified and 16 treated as ineligible cases. Out of the identified cases, 656 eligible cases are paid ex gratia, worth Rs.6,56,10,000.

The number of missing cases reported in this district are 1,683 and Rs.76,75,000 were paid ex gratia to 1,535 eligible cases.

In the district as a whole, 288 seriously injured cases were reported and an amount of Rs.27,56,000 was paid as exgratia. In the same way, Rs. 12,22,000 was paid for 617 simple injury cases.

The field data with regard to the selected mandals in Amalapuram Revenue Division are being presented in Table 4.1.

In Amalapuram mandal, deaths and missing cases are not reported in the selected sample. But there are two seriously injured cases (one male and the other female). In Ambajipeta, one female death is reported along with 8 injury cases. Among them, 4 males and one female are seriously injured and 2 males and one female are reported with simple injuries.

In I. Polavaram mandal, 94 deaths are reported. Among the 94 death cases, 34 are males, 57 are females and 2 are male children.

In Ainavilli mandal, 28 deaths are reported. Among them, 15 cases are males, 11 are females along with one male and one female child. In this mandal, one male missing case and 15 injury cases are reported. All the 15 are seriously injured.

In Katrenikona, 33 death cases are reported. Among them, 23 are males, and 12 females, along with 8 are children. There are 7 missing cases and 14 seriously injured cases.

Table 4.1: Damage to Lives.

Mandal	*Number of Injured*					*Number of Deaths*					*Number of Missing*					*Overall*
	Adults		*Children*			*Adults*		*Children*			*Adults*		*Children*			*Total*
	M	F	M	F	T	M	F	M	F	T	M	F	M	F	T	
Amalapuram	1	1	0	0	2	0	0	0	0	0	0	0	0	0	0	2
Ambajipeta	6	2	0	0	8	0	1	0	0	1	0	0	0	0	0	9
I. Polavaram	0	0	0	0	0	34	57	2	1	94	0	0	0	0	0	94
Ainavilli	3	5	0	0	8	15	11	1	1	28	1	0	0	0	1	37
Katrenikona	10	4	0	0	14	23	12	3	5	33	5	2	0	0	7	64
Total	**20**	**12**	**0**	**0**	**32**	**72**	**81**	**6**	**7**	**166**	**6**	**2**	**0**	**0**	**8**	**206**

(Figures in parentheses indicate percentages)

Dead bodies of victims horizontally placed in an area for identification

Dead bodies dumped together at one place on the sea-coast

The stinking dead body of a woman thrown aside by the flood getting stuck to the ground on the sea-coast

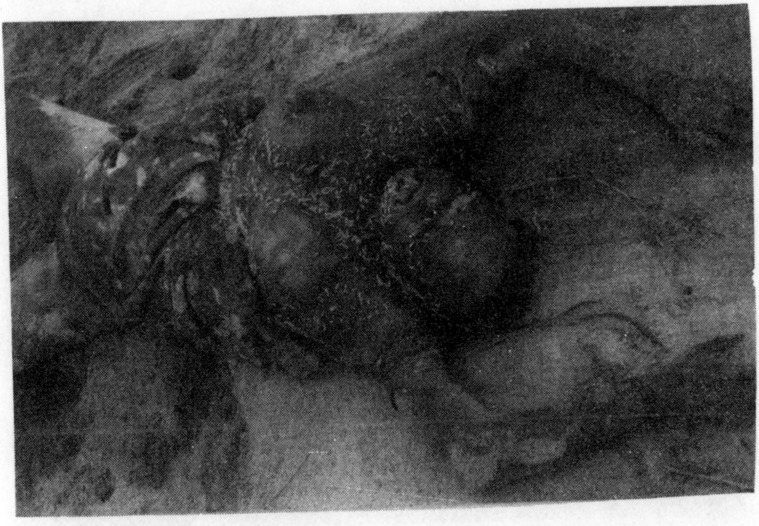

A women's dead body thrown aside by the flood, got stuck to the sand beach stinking at the sea-cost, warms-covered

The dead body of a victim stuck to sand on the coast during the flood

The dead body of a victim stuck to sand on the coast during the flood

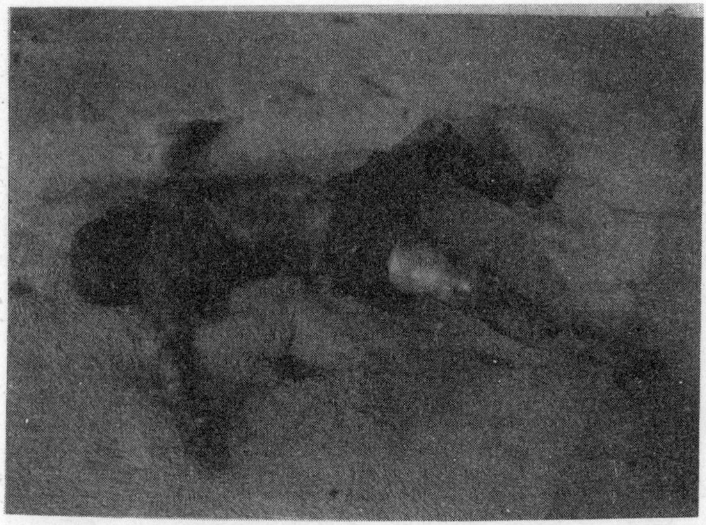

The dead body of a boy from the nearby village under the impact of cyclone

An Indian Soldier with a long pole pulling the dead bodies for identification

After the disaster burning of carcasses of victims

A sorrowful view of a submerged victim lying among the sea weeds and creepers by the sea-coast

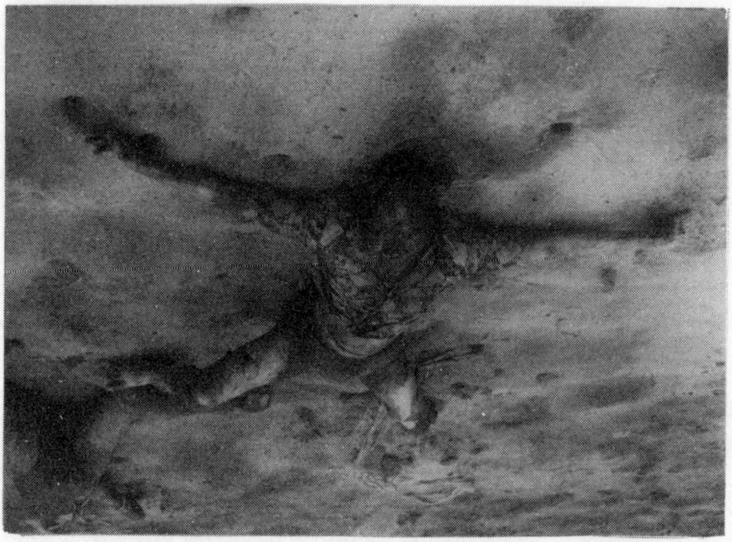

The dead body of a victim lying on the sea-coast

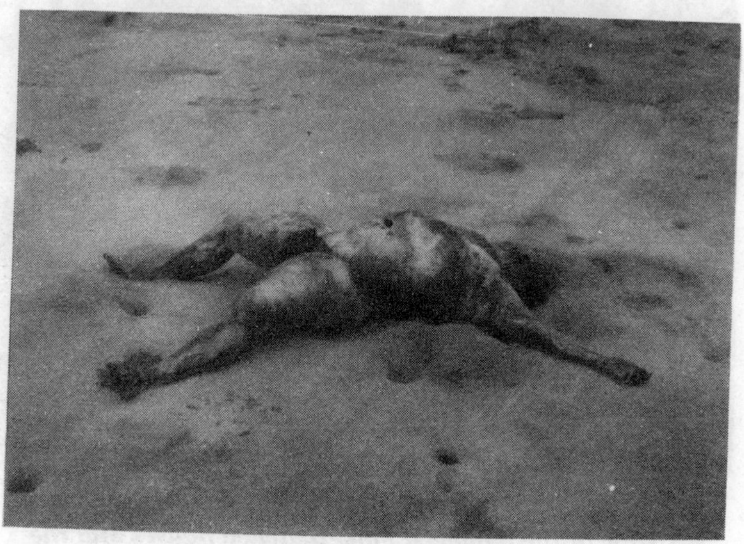

A ghastly scene on the sea-coast

A woman drowned into the flood and thrown aside on the sea-coast

A view of the damaged huts, thatched houses and the coconut trees being visited by the Health Minister, Dr. Metla Satyanarayana, during past-cyclone period

A Villagers at work on the uprooted coconut trees and other useful trees under the cyclone impact while the Government Official's look during at their visit

Complete damaged banana plants during cyclone

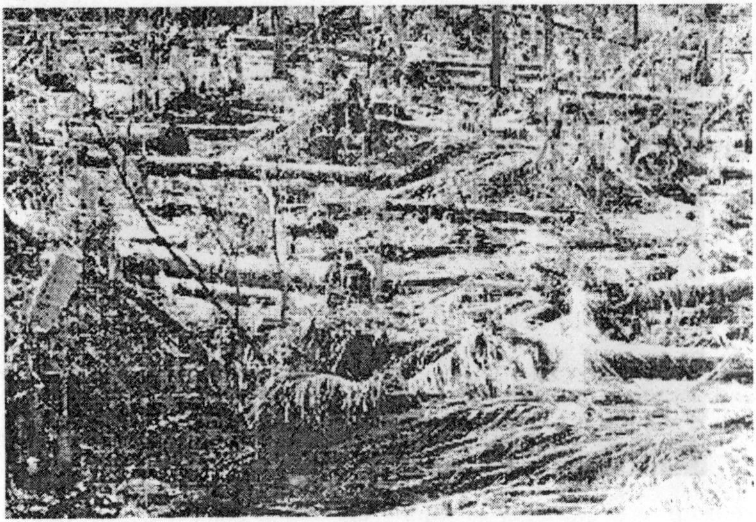

The coconut trees completely uprooted in the garden nearby sea-shore

The coconut trees completely uprooted except small saplings

The overall scenario of damage to lives shows that there are 166 death cases out of which male cases are 72, female cases 81 and 13 are children. The number of missing cases are only 8 in this sample. There are 32 injury cases. The mandal-wise analysis shows that more deaths are reported in I. Polavaram, Ainavilli and Katrenikona.

I. Polavaram topped with 94 death cases, Katrenikona topped with more injury cases (14) along with more missing cases (7). More number of female deaths are reported in I. Polavaram mandal and, on the whole, there are more number of female deaths also.

Damage to Property

Damage here includes damage to houses, damage to petty shops, damage to crops, damage to fishermen's equipment, damage to livestock etc.

As per the damage assessment in the East Godavari District, the recorded house damages were 4,43,107. Out of them, 2,58,389 were fully damaged and 1,84,718 partly damaged. As per G.O. Ms. No. 801 dt.27.9.96, Rs.1000/- plus Rs.200/- (for utensils and clothes) per fully damaged house and Rs.500/- plus (Rs.200/- for utensils and clothes) per house to partly damaged ones was paid as relief.

In the district, 10,192 petty shops were damaged. The damaged petty shops were paid relief amount of Rs.86,47,000, at the rate of Rs.1000/- per shop.

East Godavari District, particularly Konaseema is famous for growing coconut trees besides paddy. In the district total damaged cropped area under Paddy is 1,65,348 hectares and 3,00,791 small and marginal farmers were fully affected. The extent of damage to coconut plantations was 90,832 acres and 2,32,754 coconut farmers were fully affected.

As per Ref. A10. 18077/96 dt.8.11.96 of the Collector, East Godavari, the agriculture input subsidy was paid at the rate Rs.625/- per hectare which is accounted for a total amount of Rs.7,24,93,125/- towards seeds, fertilizers and pesticides. The damage assessment was recorded in three categories i.e., Category I->75 per cent damage, Category-II-50 per cent damage to 75 per cent damage and Category-III-<50 per cent damage.

In the entire district, the Konaseema is famous for growing of coconut trees after the State of Kerala in the country and it was badly affected. The coconut damages were recorded in three forms: (i) uprooted; (ii) broken; (iii) crown damaged. The severity is more among the 8 coastal mandals of the district. Those are: (1) Allavaram, (2) Mamidikuduru, (3) Uppalaguptam, (4) Katrenikona, (5) I. Polavaram, (6) Mummidivaram, (7) Ainavilli, and (8) Ambajipeta. As per Damage Assessment Committee indication, an extent of 90,932 acres was covered by damages to 2,32,754 farmers. The total number of partially affected trees were 43,54,459 and 28,07,229 trees were fully affected. As per G.O. Ms. No. 1043 Rev. dept. dt.10.12.96 and G.O. Ms. No.58 dt.25.02.97, compensation was paid @ Rs.150/- per fully damaged plant and @ Rs.50/- per partly damaged plant subject to the limitation of 60 plants per acre.

Other crops like Banana, Vegetables, Guava, Mango, Cashew, Orange, Betelleaves, and Chillies were also damaged. As per Damage Assessment Committee indication, an extent of 1,281 acres of Cashew, 1,381 acres of Mango, 1,476 acres of Guava, 280 acres of Sapota, 686 acres of Citrus fruits, 23,248 acres of Banana, 105 acres of flowers and 190 acres of other crops were affected with above 50 per cent damage.

Number of fishermen who were affected by loss of boats, crafts and tackles were 18,685. As per East Godavari Collector's A.10/87/96, dt.8.11.96, Rs.1,23,87,200/- relief was paid to affected fishermen.

The following Tables present the data with regard to damage to property and damage to crops:

Table 4.2: Damage to Property.

Mandal	*Live stock*	*Land*	*House*	*Loss in Rupees*
Amalapuram	50,700 (1.4)	2,179,500 (60.6)	1,365,000 (38.0)	3,595,200 (100.0)
Ambajipeta	1,62,400 (3.4)	2,848,000 (60.4)	1,701,000 (36.2)	4,711,400 (100.0)
I. Polavaram	1,69,820 (1.6)	7,162,000 (67.8)	3,230,500 (30.6)	10,562,320 (100.0)
Ainavilli	4,49,350 (5.8)	4,722,100 (61.2)	2,544,200 (33.0)	7,715,650 (100.0)
Katrenikona	7,10,300 (7.8)	2,390,000 (26.2)	6,021,000 (66.0)	9,121,300 (100.0)
Total	**1,542,570** **(4.3)**	**19,301,600** **(54.1)**	**14,861,700** **(41.6)**	**35,705,870** **(100.0)**

(Figures in parentheses indicate percentages)

Table-4.2 presents the data of the extent of damage to land property during the cyclone which includes damage to crops as well as damage to land due to siltation. In Amalapuram, the loss of property is Rs.3,595,200. Out of that, the loss of livestock is one per cent, loss in land is 61 per cent and 38 per cent of loss due to house damages.

In Ambajipeta, the loss in livestock is 3 per cent, the loss in land is 60 per cent, the loss in House property is 36 per cent and the total loss in Ambajipeta is Rs.4,711,400.

In I. Polavaram, the total loss is Rs.10,562,320. The loss in livestock is one per cent, the loss in land is 67.8 per cent, and the loss in house is 30.6 per cent.

In Ainavilli, out of the total loss of Rs.7,715,600, the loss in livestock is 6 per cent, the loss in land is 61 per cent and the loss in house is 33 per cent.

In Katrenikona, the total loss is Rs.9,121,300. Out of that, the loss in livestock is 8 per cent, the loss in land is 26 per cent and the loss in house property is 66 per cent.

Overall, the loss is Rs.35,75,870 in the sample villages. Out of that, the loss in livestock is 4 per cent, the loss in land is 54 per cent and the loss due to house damages is 42 per cent. On the whole, the loss in livestock and house damages are the highest in the Katrenikona mandal, and the damage to land is more in I. Polavaram mandal. In Katrenikona, being a economically backward mandal, most of the respondents in this mandal are dependent on fishing, the loss in land is one-fourth whereas in other four mandals the loss in land is nearly two-thirds.

Table 4.3 presents the data with regard to damage to crops. In Amalapuram mandal, the maximum damage with 70 per cent is to coconut plantations, out of the total loss of Rs.2,006,500. In this mandal, the loss to Paddy is 17 per cent, one per cent loss to Vegetables and 11 per cent loss to Bananas.

In Ambajipeta mandal, out of the total loss of Rs.2,803,000, the maximum loss (68 per cent) is to coconut plantations, with 17 per cent loss to Bananas, 9 per cent loss to Vegetables and 6 per cent loss to Paddy.

In I. Polavaram mandal, the total loss is in 5,052,000. Out of that, the loss to Paddy is 53 per cent, loss to coconut plantations is 47 per cent and there is only 0.4 per cent loss to Bananas.

In Ainavilli mandal, the loss to coconut plantations is with 53 per cent out of the total loss of Rs.3,663,600. The loss to Paddy is 35 per cent and 4 per cent loss to Vegetables.

In Katrenikona mandal, out of the total loss of Rs.2,045,000, the loss to coconut plantations is 51 per cent, loss to paddy 49 per cent and a minute loss to Vegetables.

The overall scenario of Damage to crops shows that there is more loss to coconut plantations with 56 per cent, out of the total loss of Rs.15,570,100. Next comes the loss

Table 4.3: Damage to Crops.

Mandal	*Paddy*	*Coconuts*	*Vegetables*	*Chillies*	*Tobacco*	*Banana*	*Loss in Rupees*
Amalapuram	346,000(17.2)	1,411,000(70.3)	21,000(1.0)	0(0.0)	0(0.0)	228,500(11.4)	2,006,500 (100.0
Ambajipeta	165,000(5.9)	1,891,000(67.5)	2,57,000(9.2)	0(0.0)	0(0.0)	4,90,000(17.4)	2,803,000(100.0)
I. Polavaram	2,677,000(53.0)	2,355,000(46.6)	0(0.0)	0(0.0)	0(0.0)	20,000(0.4)	5,052,000(100.0)
Ainavilli	12,65,500(34.5)	1,942,600(53.0)	1,56,000(4.3)	0(0.0)	0(0.0)	2,99,500(8.2)	3,663,600(100.0)
Katrenikona	1,009,000(49.3)	1,035,000(50.6)	1,000(0.04)	0(0.0)	0(0.0)	0(0.0)	2,045,000(100.0)
Total	**5,462,500(35.1)**	**8,634,600(55.5)**	**435,000(2.8)**	**0(0.0)**	**0(0.0)**	**1,038,000(6.6)**	**15,570,100(100.0)**

(Figures in parentheses indicate percentages)

to Paddy with 35 per cent, with 3 per cent loss to vegetables and 7 per cent loss to Bananas. Compared to other mandals, the loss to coconut plantations is more in Amalapuram and Ambajipeta mandals. In I. Polavaram mandal, the loss to paddy is more while Katrenikona the loss to Paddy and coconut plantations is almost equal.

On the whole, the coconut plantations in Konaseema are badly affected during the Cyclone and also caused heavy losses to other crops as well as to their lands. To evacuate the fallen trees and to restore their lands it took a lot of time and money.

Loss of Essential Commodities to Households

In the entire district as per the Government's wireless message No.58040 (Relief-1) 96, dt.22/23.10.96, besides organizing the relief camps, the authorities immediately distributed 25 kg of rice to all the households with their houses fully damaged irrespective of their economic background. Besides, 3 liters of kerosene was distributed in the I phase and later 5 liters of kerosene was distributed to all the families. The total rice of 17,528 M.Ts and 4,611 K.Ls of kerosene oil were distributed to 7,35,140 affected families. And also an amount of Rs.26,84,500 was paid to 5,369 weavers in the district for loom and yarn damages.

Socio-economic Infrastructural damages

In view of the unprecedented impact of cyclone, extensive damages had been caused to almost all the Departments like Irrigation, Roads and Buildings, Medical & Health, Drainage, Panchayat Raj, A.P.S.E.B., Telecommunications, A.P.S.R.T.C. etc. The Government had released Rs.6 crores to take up immediate restoration works and the amount was allotted among the following Departments' Rs.13.3 lakhs to Irrigation Department, Rs.115 lakhs to Municipalities, Rs.157 crores to Panchayat Raj, Rs.166 crores to Roads and Buildings, Rs.3 lakhs to Drainage, Rs.0.17 lakh to Social Welfare and Rs.25 lakhs to A.P.S.E.B. under the aegis of the NABARD and the World Bank for the restoration of socio-economic infrastructures.

Part-C

Rescue, Relief and Rehabilitation Operations

Because of cyclone, extensive damages have been caused in most of the Mandals. Hence, the following action has been initiated to provide relief:

1. All trees which fell down causing obstruction to general public on the roads should be removed by route-wise teams and ensure that communications are restored. Gram Panchayats were authorised to take away the wood and conduct auction for the clearance of debris and removal of all obstructions. In case the Gram Panchayats were not readily forthcoming local individuals may be encouraged to remove so that A.P.S.R.T.C. shall be given obstacle-free roads to ply buses.

2. On a large scale, carcasses which lay unattended, should be removed and burnt by local Panchayats with the assistance of Police. The Mandal Revenue Officers will arrange Diesel/Kerosene oil free of cost for this purpose and the Mandal Revenue Officers may claim necessary reimbursements later on.

3. Mandal Revenue Officers have to take initiatives to arrange distribution of free food packets without giving scope to any complaint, to all the families evacuated and for all the families marooned in the cyclonic rain-water. The Mandal Revenue Officers were also given powers to distribute 25 kgs of rice to the affected families irrespective of the income limit.

4. The Revenue Divisional Officers were authorised to draw and disburse ex gratia @Rs.50,000/- as

Chief Minister's Relief fund to the next of kin of each deceased person because of the cyclonic storm.

5. For speedy distribution of relief the Mandal Revenue Officers of the district have been authorized to draw and disburse monetary relief, additional relief (clothes/utensils) and Rice (for affected families towards house damages and affected weavers' families)
6. In addition to the existing staff engaged in relief measures nearly 500 members from various Departments and other districts were already deployed for enumeration of damages and for attending on relief operations.
7. The Commander Coastal Guard, Visakhapatnam were already requested to make searches for tracing out fishermen who have missed in the sea.
8. Three helicopters of the Indian Navy have been stationed at Rajahmundry for air dropping of bread dry food and large quantity of bamboos and water in the affected areas.
9. The Forest Department had already opened retail sale depots for the supply of bamboo etc., to the Cyclone victims.
10. Nine cranes and two proclainers were received from the Deputy Transport Commissioner, Visakhapatnam which were deployed in Amalapuram division for clearing out obstacles.
11. A total number of 113 vehicles of various types, viz., lorries, buses, cabs and goods-vehicles etc., were requistioned for cyclone relief operations and were sent to various mandals affected in the district.
12. Instructions were issued to all the Mandal Revenue Officers to supply 3 liters of Kerosene oil to all the affected families free of cost.

Source: My Experiences with Hurricane

Productivity Opinions on Crops

The respondents were questioned for their opinions about the productivity of crops after the Cyclone. Table 4.4 presents the distribution of data with regard to productivity of crops.

Table 4.4: Opinions on productivity of crops.

Mandal	*Satisfied*	*Partially Satisfied*	*Dissatisfied*	*Not Relevant*	*Total Respondents*
Amalapuram	0(0.0)	48(56.5)	13(15.3)	24(15.3)	85(100.0)
Ambajipeta	0(0.0)	41(52.6)	26(33.3)	11(14.1)	78(100.0)
I. Polavaram	0(0.0)	44(33.6)	37(28.2)	50(38.2)	131(100.0)
Ainavilli	0(0.0)	99(61.0)	64(39.0)	0(0.0)	163(100.0)
Katrenikona	1(0.7)	66(46.3)	41(28.7)	35(24.5)	143(100.0)
Total	**1(0.1)**	**298(49.7)**	**181(30.2)**	**120(20.0)**	**600(100.0)**

(Figures in parentheses indicate percentages)

The respondents who are having fields and coconut plantations are asked for their opinions. The landless respondents are put in the category of not relevant. Not only the respondents with agriculture as their main occupation, but also respondents with other occupations also have landed property, e.g., All the respondents in Government service are having land-holdings.

In Amalapuram, out of 85 respondents, 57 per cent opined that they are partially satisfied and 15 per cent opined that they are dissatisfied with the productivity of crops after the Cyclone.

In Ambajipeta, out of the 78 respondents, 53 per cent are partially satisfied and 33 per cent are dissatisfied with their crops. In I. Polavaram, out of 131 respondents, 34 per cent are partially satisfied and 28 per cent are dissatisfied. In Ainavilli mandal, out of 163 respondents, 61 per cent are partially satisfied and 39 per cent are dissatisfied. In Katrenikona, out of 143 respondents, one respondent is satisfied, half of the respondents are only partially satisfied and 29 per cent are dissatisfied with the productivity of their crops.

On the whole, half of the respondents are only partially satisfied with 30 per cent totally dissatisfied and only one respondent satisfied with the productivity of their crops after the cyclone. Overall, 20 per cent are in not-relevant category. Interestingly, in Ainavilli mandal, all the respondents have lands including the 41 per cent agricultural labourers (mostly they are small and marginal formers). The above data show that the cyclone had drastically affected the productivity of crops.

Restoration

When the respondents are questioned about restoration, some told that they are restored and some told that they are not yet restored. The distribution of restoration data is presented in Table-4.5:

Table 4.5: Restoration.

Mandal	*Restored*	*Not Restored*	*Total Respondents*
Amalapuram	45(52.9)	40(47.1)	85(100.0)
Ambajipeta	20(25.6)	58(74.4)	78(100.0)
I. Polavaram	126(96.2)	5(3.8)	131(100.0)
Ainavilli	151(92.6)	12(7.4)	163(100.0)
Katrenikona	87(60.8)	56(39.2)	143(100.0)
Total	**429(71.5)**	**171(28.5)**	**600(100.0)**

(Figures in parentheses indicate percentages)

The above Table-4.5 shows that, in Amalapuram mandal, out of 85 respondents, 53 per cent opined as restored and 47 per cent said as not restored. In Ambajipeta mandal, out of 78 respondents, only 26 per cent opined as restored and majority (74 per cent) opined as not restored. In I. Polavaram mandal, out of 131 respondents, majority (96 per cent) opined as restored and only a minority (4 per cent) opined as not restored. In

Ainavilli mandal also, out of 163 respondents, majority (93 per cent) opined as restored and only 7 per cent opined as not restored. In Katrenikona mandal, 61 per cent opined as restored and 39 per cent opined as not restored.

On the whole, the data show that majority (71.5 per cent) opined as restored and 28.5 per cent opined as not restored. In I. Polavaram and Ainavilli mandals, majority opined as restored. The position of Amalapuram and Katrenikona mandals is also not so much bad. But in Ambajipeta mandal, three-fourths of the respondents opined as not restored.

Time taken for Restoration to original Position: Overall 429 respondents opined as restored in the total sample of 600. They are asked further for the time required to get their original position.

Table 4.6: Time taken for Restoration to Original Position.

Mandal	*<=3 Months*	*>3 Months and<=6 Months*	*>6 Months and <=11 Months*	*<=2 Years*	*>2 Years*	*Total Respondents*
Amalapuram	0(0.0)	11(24.4)	2(4.4)	29(64.4)	3(6.8)	45(100.0)
Ambajipeta	3(1.5)	1(5.0)	0(0.0)	13(65.0)	3(15.0)	20(100.0)
I. Polavaram	10(7.9)	101(80.2)	11(8.7)	4(3.2)	0(0.0)	126(100.0)
Ainavilli	20(13.2)	41(27.2)	4(2.6)	57(37.7)	29(19.3)	151(100.0)
Katrenikona	19(21.8)	38(43.7)	4(4.6)	22(25.3)	4(4.6)	87(100.0)
Total	**52(12.1)**	**192(44.8)**	**21(4.9)**	**125(29.1)**	**39(9.1)**	**429(100.0)**

(Figures in parentheses indicate percentages)

Table-4.6 presents the data of time taken to get normalcy. In Amalapuram mandal, out of 45 opined as restored, 24 per cent told that 3-6 moths time was required, 4 per cent told that 6 months to one year time was required, 64 per cent told that 1-2 years time was required and 7 per cent told that more than 2 years time was required to get to their normal position.

In Ambajipeta mandal, out of 20 opined as restored, majority (65 per cent) opined that it takes 1-2 years time, another 15 per cent opined that it takes more than 2 years to get normalcy and only 20 per cent opined that it takes less then 6 months time.

In I. Polavaram mandal, out of 126 opined as restored, majority (80 per cent) opinied as 3-6 months time is required to get normal position, 8 per cent hold as less than 3 months, 9 per cent hold 6 months to one year and 3 per cent hold 1-2 years time to get original position.

In Ainavilli mandal, out of 151 opined as restored, 13 per cent hold as less than 3 months time, 27 per cent 3-6 months time, 3 percent 6 months to one year time, 38 per cent 1-2 years time and 19 per cent more than 2 years time to get normalcy.

In Katrenikona mandal, out of 87 opined as restored, 22 per cent hold as less than 3 months time to restore, 44 per cent 3-6 months time, 5 per cent 6 months to one year, 25 per cent 1-2 years time and 5 per cent more than 2 years time to restore to normalcy.

On the whole, out of 429 total who opined as restored, 12 per cent hold as less than 3 months time, 45 per cent 3-6 months time, 5 per cent 6 months to one year time, 29 per cent 1-2 years time and 9 per cent required more than 2 years time to get normalcy. Overall, among those who opined as restored, majority (45 per cent) hold as 3-6 months time to restore. Compared to other mandals, in I. Polavaram majority of the respondents (88 per cent) hold as less than six months time to restore. More respondents (19 per cent) in Ainavilli mandal hold as took more than 2 years time to restore, compared to other mandals.

Money spent for Restoration

It is observed that lot of money was spent by the 600 respondents to restore. But some are not yet restored. The total money spent (the sources of money are categorized into self, loan and aid) is structured and the categories of respondents are presented in the Table-4.7.

Table-4.7 presents the distribution of respondents based on money spent for restoration. In Amalapuram mandal, out of 85 respondents, 14 per cent spent less then Rs.10,000, majority (65 per cent) spent Rs.10,000-20,000, 13 per cent spent Rs.20,000-30,000, one per cent spent Rs.30,000-40,000 and 7 per cent spent Rs.50,000 and more to restore to original positions.

In Ambajipeta mandal, out of 78 respondents, 15 per cent spent less than Rs.10,000, 33 per cent spent Rs.10,000-20,000, 27 per cent spent Rs.20,000-30,000, 5 per cent spent Rs.30,000-40,000, one per cent spent Rs.40,000-50,000 and 18 per cent spent Rs.50,000 and more to restore to original positions.

In I. Polavaram mandal, out of 131 respondents, 8 per cent spent less than Rs.10,000, 21 per cent each spent Rs.10,000-20,000 and Rs.20,000-30,000, 17 per cent spent Rs.30,000-40,000, 12 per cent spent Rs.40,000-50,000 and 22 per cent spent Rs.50,000 and more to restore to original positions.

In Ainavilli mandal, 36 per cent spent less than Rs.10,000, 26 per cent spent Rs.10,000-20,000, 10 per cent spent Rs.20,000-30,000, 3 per cent spent Rs.30,000-40,000, 7 per cent spent Rs.40,000-50,000 and 8 per cent spent Rs.50,000 and more to restore to original positions.

In Katrenikona mandal, out of 143 respondents, 7 per cent spent less than Rs.10,000, 26 per cent each spent Rs.10,000-20,000 and Rs.20,000-30,000, 11 per cent spent Rs.30,000-40,000, 9 per cent spent Rs.40,000-50,000 and 21 per cent spent Rs.50,000 and more to restore to original positions.

On the whole, out of 600 respondents, 17 per cent spent less than Rs.10,000, majority (34 per cent) spent

Table 4.7: Money spent for Restoration.

Mandal	*<10,000*	*10,000-20,000*	*20,000-30,000*	*30,000-40,000*	*40,000-50,000*	*>=50,000*	*Total Respondents*
Amalapuram	12(14.1)	55(64.7)	11(12.9)	1(1.2)	0(0.0)	6(7.1)	85(100.0)
Ambajipeta	12(15.4)	26(33.3)	21(26.9)	4(5.1)	1(1.3)	14(18.0)	78(100.0)
I. Polavaram	11(8.4)	27(20.6)	27(20.6)	22(16.8)	15(11.5)	29(22.1)	131(100.0)
Ainavilli	59(36.2)	58(35.6)	17(10.4)	5(3.1)	11(6.7)	13(8.0)	163(100.0)
Katrenikona	10(6.9)	37(25.9)	37(25.9)	16(11.2)	13(9.1)	30(21.0)	143(100.0)
Total	**104(17.3)**	**203(33.8)**	**113(18.8)**	**48(8.0)**	**40(6.7)**	**92(15.4)**	**600(100.0)**

(Figures in parentheses indicate percentages)

Rs.10,000-20,000, 19 per cent spent Rs.20,000-30,000, 8 per cent spent Rs.30,000-40,000, 7 per cent spent Rs.40,000-50,000 and 15 per cent spent Rs.50,000 and more to restore to original positions. Overall, the respondents that spent less than Rs.10,000/- are more in Ainavilli mandal (36 per cent) than in other mandals. In the same way, more number of respondents in I. Polavaram and Katrenikona mandals spent Rs.50,000 and more than in other mandals.

Note

In Katrenikona mandal, majority of the respondents (66 per cent), fall in the total household Income category of Rs.5,000-15,000, and there are no respondents in the highest income groups of Rs.45,000-65,000. But interestingly, when we refer to Table-4.7, 30 per cent of the respondents in Katrenikona spent Rs.40,000-50,000 and even more to get their original positions. The reason is that, in Katrenikona, the damage to house property is more than in other mandals, which includes, houses, agricultural implements, fishermen's equipment like boats, nets, crafts, tackles, other household articles, gold etc., with damage to livestock also is more in this mandal. The number of deaths is also more in this mandal. The fishermen community in this mandal are badly affected. There were more deaths and they lost costly fishing equipment. It is noticed that the authorities (Central, State & Voluntary Organisations) concentrated more on fishing villages after the cyclone. They gave ex gratia to the dead, missing and injured cases, with loans distributed by voluntary organizations in thousands of rupees to purchase and repair fishing equipment with aid also being more in these villages as all the above distributed aid is more in this village. But this is not the case with other villages. (Refer Tables-4.8, 4.9 & 4.10). Another noticeable point is that gold rescues individuals in times of need, and people buy gold when there is money and when need arises, they can sell it. And gold doesn't come under total Household income.

Money Spent for Restoration (self)

Table-4.8 presents the data with regard to money spent by the respondent for restoration. The question is asked as to know how much he spent on his own finances.

Table 4.8: Money spent for restoration-[Self].

Mandal	*<10,000*	*10,000-20,000*	*20,000-30,000*	*30,000-40,000*	*40,000-50,000*	*>= 50,000*	*Total Respondents*
Amalapuram	21 (24.7)	50 (59.0)	8 (9.4)	3 (3.5)	1 (1.2)	2 (2.2)	85 (100.0)
Ambajipeta	19 (24.4)	28 (35.9)	17 (21.8)	3 (3.8)	2 (2.6)	9 (11.5)	78 (100.0)
I. Polavaram	64 (48.9)	35 (26.7)	27 (20.6)	2 (1.5)	3 (2.3)	0 (0.0)	131 (100.0)
Ainavilli	128 (78.5)	27 (16.6)	5 (3.1)	1 (0.6)	1 (0.6)	1 (0.6)	163 (100.0)
Katrenikona	56 (39.2)	55 (38.5)	21 (14.7)	5 (3.5)	2 (1.4)	4 (2.7)	143 (100.0)
Total	**288** **(48.0)**	**195** **(32.5)**	**78** **(13.0)**	**14** **(2.3)**	**9** **(1.5)**	**16** **(2.7)**	**600** **(100.0)**

(Figures in parentheses indicate percentages)

In Amalapuram mandal, out of 85 respondents, 25 per cent spent less than Rs.10,000, 59 per cent spent Rs.10,000-20,000, 9 per cent spent Rs.20,000-30,000, 4 per cent spent Rs.30,000-40,000, one per cent spent Rs.40,000-50,000 and 2 per cent spent Rs.50,000 and more to restructure their lives.

In Ambajipeta mandal, out of 78 respondents, 24 per cent spent less than Rs.10,000, 36 per cent spent Rs.10,000-20,000, 22 per cent spent Rs.20,000-30,000, 4 per cent spent Rs.30,000-40,000, 3 per cent spent Rs.40,000-50,000 and 12 per cent spent Rs.50,000 and more to restructure their lives.

In I. Polavaram mandal, out of 131 respondents, 49 per cent spent less than Rs.10,000, 27 per cent spent

Rs.10,000-20,000, 21 per cent spent Rs.20,000-30,000, 2 per cent each spent Rs.30,000-40,000 and Rs.40,000-50,000 to restructure their lives.

In Ainavilli mandal, out of 163 respondents, 79 per cent spent less than Rs.10,000, 17 per cent spent Rs.10,000-20,000, 3 per cent spent Rs.20,000-30,000, about 2 per cent spent Rs.30,000-50,000 and more from their pockets to restore themselves.

In Katrenikona mandal, out of 143 respondents, 42 per cent spent less than Rs.10,000, 40 per cent spent Rs.10,000-20,000, 15 per cent spent Rs.20,000-30,000, and only 4 per cent spent Rs.30,000-40,000 from their finances to restore themselves.

On the whole, out of 600 respondents, majority (48 per cent) spent less than Rs.10,000, 33 per cent spent Rs.10,000-20,000, 13 per cent spent Rs.20,000-30,000, 2 per cent each spent Rs.30,000-40,000 and Rs.40,000-50,000 and only 3 per cent spent Rs.50,000 and more from their finances to restructure themselves. The overall scenario shows that only in Ambajipeta mandal, respondents spent Rs.50,000 and more on their own, when compared to other mandals. In Katrenikona mandal, there are more respondents who, while looking from the angle of total household income, nearly half of them spent less than Rs.10,000 from their pockets to restore themselves. This corroborates with their low socio-economic background, as is already mentioned in the last chapter.

Money Spent for Restoration-Loan

As about the loan money spent for Restoration, from the sources of loans-from Banks, from moneylenders, from Co-operative Societies, from Voluntary Organizations etc., the data about the opinions of the respondents is presented in Table-4.9.

Table 4.9: Money spent for restoration-Loans.

Mandal	*<10,000*	*10,000-20,000*	*20,000-30,000*	*30,000-40,000*	*40,000-50,000*	*>= 50,000*	*Total Respondents*
Amalapuram	71 (83.5)	9 (10.6)	2 (2.3)	1 (1.2)	1 (1.2)	1 (1.2)	85 (100.0)
Ambajipeta	61 (78.2)	6 (7.7)	6 (7.7)	2 (2.6)	1 (1.3)	2 (2.5)	78 (100.0)
I. Polavaram	45 (34.3)	34 (26.0)	22 (17.0)	9 (7.0)	6 (5.0)	15 (11.5)	131 (100.0)
Ainavilli	86 (52.7)	45 (47.6)	9 (5.5)	7 (4.3)	6 (3.7)	10 (6.2)	163 (100.0)
Katrenikona	27 (18.9)	57 (39.9)	19 (13.3)	16 (11.2)	4 (2.8)	20 (13.9)	143 (100.0)
Total	**290 (48.3)**	**151 (25.2)**	**58 (9.7)**	**35 (5.8)**	**18 (3.0)**	**48 (8.0)**	**600 (100.0)**

(Figures in parentheses indicate percentages)

In Amalapuram mandal, out of 85 respondents, majority (83.5 per cent) spent less than Rs.10,000, 11 per cent spent Rs.10,000-20,000, 2 per cent spent Rs.20,000-30,000, one per cent each spent Rs.30,000-40,000, Rs.40,000-50,000 and Rs.50,000 and more, from the sources of loans.

In Ambajipeta mandal, out of 78 respondents, majority (78 per cent) spent less than Rs.10,000, 8 per cent each spent Rs.10,000-20,000 and Rs.20,000-30,000, 3 per cent spent Rs.30,000-40,000, one per cent spent Rs.40,000-50,000 and 3 per cent spent Rs.50,000 and more from the sources of loan.

In I. Polavaram mandal, out of 131 respondents, 34 per cent spent less than Rs.10,000, 26 per cent spent Rs.10,000-20,000, 17 per cent spent Rs.20,000-30,000, 7 per cent spent Rs.30,000-40,000, 5 per cent spent Rs.40,000-50,000 and 12 per cent spent Rs.50,000 and more from the sources of loans.

In Ainavilli mandal, out of 163 respondents, 53 per cent spent less than Rs.10,000, 48 per cent spent Rs.10,000-

20,000, 6 per cent spent Rs.20,000-30,000, 4 per cent each spent Rs.30,000-40,000 and Rs.40,000-50,000 and 6 per cent spent Rs.50,000 and more from the sources of loans.

In Katrenikona mandal, out of 143 respondents, only 19 per cent spent less than Rs.10,000, 40 per cent spent Rs.10,000-20,000, 13 per cent spent Rs.20,000-30,000, 11 per cent spent Rs.30,000-40,000, 3 per cent spent Rs.40,000-50,000 and 14 per cent spent Rs.50,000 and more from the sources of loans.

On the whole, out of 600 respondents, majority (48 per cent) spent less than Rs.10,000, 25 per cent spent Rs.10,000-20,000, 10 per cent spent Rs.20,000-30,000, 6 per cent spent Rs.30,000-40,000 3 per cent spent Rs.40,000-50,000 and 8 per cent spent Rs.50,000 and more from the sources of loans. Relatively, respondents from I. Polavaram, Ainavilli and Katrenikona mandals spent more from the sources of loans than in the other two mandals. Relief and Rehabilitation operations are more in these mandals because of high casualties.

Money Spent for Restoration Aid

Table-4.10 presents the data with regard to the amounts sanctioned by the Central, State and Voluntary Organizations to the affected victims. The amount varies from Rs.700-Rs.2,300 and more. Majority of the respondents got aid from the State Government worth of Rs.700, whereas the relief activities of the Central Government and Voluntary Organizations concentrated more on the villages where more number of casualties occurred.

In Amalapuram mandal, out of 85 respondents, majority (46 per cent) got aid worth Rs.700-1100 and 17 per cent received Rs.1100-1500.

In Ambajipeta mandal, out of 78 respondents, 12 per cent received aid of Rs.700/- majority (85 per cent) received aid of Rs.700-1100, 3 per cent received aid of Rs.1100-1500 and one per cent received aid of Rs.1500-1900.

Table 4.10: Money spent for Restoration-[Aid].

Mandal	*<900*	*900-1100*	*1100-1500*	*1500-1900*	*1900-2300*	*>=2300*	*Total Respondents*
Amalapuram	39	32	14	0	0	0	85
	(45.9)	(37.6)	(16.5)	(0.0)	(0.0)	(0.0)	
Ambajipeta	9	66	2	1	0	0	78
	(11.5)	(84.6)	(2.6)	(1.3)	(0.0)	(0.0)	
I. Polavaram	3	87	0	0	3	38	131
	(2.3)	(66.4)	(0.0)	(0.0)	(2.3)	(29.0)	
Ainavilli	46	33	72	5	3	4	163
	(28.2)	(20.2)	(44.2)	(3.1)	(1.8)	(2.5)	
Katrenikona	5	2	12	87	20	17	143
	(3.5)	(1.4)	(8.4)	(60.8)	(13.9)	(12.0)	
Total	**102**	**220**	**100**	**93**	**26**	**59**	**600**
	(17.0)	**(36.7)**	**(16.7)**	**(15.5)**	**(4.3)**	**(9.8)**	**(100.0)**

(Figures in parentheses indicate percentages)

In I. Polavaram mandal, out 131 respondents, 2 per cent received Rs.700, majority (66 per cent) received aid worth Rs.700-1100, 2 per cent received Rs.1900-2300 and significantly 29 per cent received Rs.2300 and more as aid amount.

In Ainavilli mandal, out of 163 respondents, 28 per cent received Rs.700/-, 20 per cent received Rs.700-1100, 44 per cent received Rs.1100-1500, 3 per cent received Rs.1500-1900, 2 per cent received Rs.1900-2300 and another 3 per cent received Rs.2,300 and more as aid amount.

In Katrenikona mandal, out of 143 respondents, 4 per cent received Rs.700, one per cent received Rs.700-1100, 8 per cent received Rs.1100-1500, majority (61 per cent) received aid worth Rs.1500-1900, 14 per cent received Rs.1900-2300 and 12 per cent received Rs.2,300 and more as aid amount.

The overall picture shows that, out of 600 respondents, 17 per cent received Rs.700, 37 per cent received aid worth Rs.700-1100, 17 per cent received Rs.1100-1500, 16 per cent received Rs.1500-1900, 4 per cent received Rs.1900-2300 and 10 per cent received aid worth Rs.2,300 and more. On the whole, the most beneficiary mandals are I. Polavaram, Ainavilli and Katrenikona. Even among these, I. Polavaram comes first, Katrenikona comes second and Ainavilli is in third position in terms of aid received and this corroborates with the number of deaths in these mandals.

Position of the Respondents after Cyclone

The respondents are asked for their opinions about the scarcity of food items, living conditions, psychological conditions during and after Cyclone, opinions about Cyclone etc. These variables are presented below one by one:

Position after Cyclone: Scarcity of Food Items

Table 4.11: Position after Cyclone-Scarcity of Food Items.

Mandal	*Food*	*Clothing*	*Water*	*Medicines*	*Money*	*Others*
Amalapuram	1 (3.7)	2 (8.7)	1 (1.0)	2 (2.8)	76 (23.0)	0 (0.0)
Ambajipeta	1 (3.7)	1 (4.3)	15 (14.7)	3 (4.3)	63 (19.13)	0 (0.0)
I. Polavaram	3 (11.1)	2 (8.7)	1 (1.0)	47 (66.2)	103 (31.2)	0 (0.0)
Ainavilli	21 (77.8)	17 (74.0)	30 (29.4)	17 (23.9)	87 (26.4)	1 (100.0)
Katrenikona	1 (3.7)	1 (4.3)	55 (53.9)	2 (2.8)	1 (0.3)	0 (0.0)
Total	**27 (100.0)**	**23 (100.0)**	**102 (100.0)**	**71 (100.0)**	**330 (100.0)**	**1 (100.0)**

(Figures in parentheses indicate percentages)

In the above Table-4.11, the respondents felt about the scarcity of food items after the Cyclone. Overall, 27 respondents felt about the scarcity of food items after the cyclone. Out of that, majority (78 per cent) in Ainavilli mandal felt about the food scarcity after cyclone.

Overall, 2.3 respondents felt the scarcity of clothing and, out of that, majority (74 per cent) in Ainavilli felt the scarcity after the cyclone. On the whole, 102 respondent felt about the water scarcity and majority (54 per cent) in Katrenikona felt about water scarcity. Next, in Ainavilli and Ambajipeta mandals, the respondents felt more about the water scarcity than in other two mandals. Overall, 71 respondents felt about scarcity of medicines. Majority (66 per cent) in I. Polavaram, and 24 per cent in Ainavilli felt mandals felt about the scarcity of medicines after the cyclone. Overall, 330 (half of the respondents) felt about the scarcity of money. Except Katrenikona, all other mandals felt about the need of money after cyclone. This shows that the respondents in Katrenikona mandal received immediate aid from the authorities.

The overall scenario shows that the respondents in Ainavilli felt about the scarcity of food items and other necessary items relatively more than the other mandals. Comparatively, the respondents in Katrenikona mandal felt less about scarcity of necessary items except water than in other mandals. Except Katrenikona, all the respondents in the four mandals felt about the need of money after cyclone. The above data show a clear picture of scarcity of important items, including money, after a natural calamity like cyclone.

Position after Cyclone: Living Conditions

Table-4.12 presents the data with regard to the living conditions of respondents after the cyclone. In Amalapuram mandal, out 85 respondents, majority (99 per cent) felt very bad about the living conditions after the Cyclone. In Ambajipeta mandal, out of 78 respondents (90 per cent) opined that the living conditions are very bad. In I. Polavaram mandal, out of 131 respondents, 64 per cent felt

Table 4.12: Position after Cyclone-[Living Conditions].

Mandal	*Good*	*Bad*	*Very Bad*	*Total Respondent*
Amalapuram	0(0.0)	1(1.2)	84(98.8)	85(100.0)
Ambajipeta	2(2.6)	6(7.7)	70(89.7)	78(100.0)
I. Polavaram	84(64.1)	22(16.8)	25(19.1)	131(100.0)
Ainavilli	38(23.3)	29(17.8)	96(58.9)	163(100.0)
Katrenikona	136(95.0)	0(0.0)	7(5.0)	143(100.0)
Total	**260(43.3)**	**58(9.7)**	**282(47.0)**	**600(100.0)**

(Figures in parentheses indicate percentages)

that the living conditions are good, 17 per cent felt that the living conditions are bad and 19 per cent felt that the living conditions are very bad. In Ainavilli mandal, out of 163 respondents, 23 per cent felt that the living conditions are good, 18 per cent felt that the living conditions are bad, and majority (59 per cent) felt that the living conditions are very bad. In Katrenikona mandal, out of 143 respondents, majority (95 per cent) felt that the living conditions are good and only 5 per cent felt that the living conditions are very bad.

On the whole, out of 600 respondents, 43 per cent felt that the living conditions are good, 10 per cent felt that the living conditions are bad and 47 per cent felt that the living conditions are very bad. Overall, the respondents in Amalapuram and Ambajipeta mandals felt that the living conditions are very bad. Even in Ainavilli mandal more than half felt that the living conditions are bad. The respondents in Katrenikona mandal are the happiest people with regard to living conditions which shows the speedy rescue and relief operations to this mandal.

Position During the Cyclone-Psychological Conditions

The psychological conditions of the respondents during the cyclone are presented in Table-4.13:

Table 4.13: Position during Cyclone-[Psychological Condition].

Mandal	*Moderate*	*Fearful*	*Very Fearful*	*Total Respondents*
Amalapuram	6(7.1)	13(15.3)	66(77.6)	85(100.0)
Ambajipeta	3(3.8)	14(17.9)	61(78.2)	78(100.0)
I. Polavaram	4(3.0)	0(0.0)	127(97.0)	131(100.0)
Ainavilli	21(12.8)	1(0.6)	141(86.6)	163(100.0)
Katrenikona	4(2.8)	23(16.1)	116(81.1)	143(100.0)
Total	**38(6.3)**	**51(8.5)**	**511(85.2)**	**600(100.0)**

(Figures in parentheses indicate percentages)

In Amalapuram mandal, out of 85 respondents, 7 per cent opined that their psychological condition is moderate, 15 per cent opined that they felt fearful and majority (78 per cent) felt the cyclone as very fearful. In Ambajipeta mandal, out of 78 respondents, 4 per cent felt the day as moderate, 18 per cent felt as fearful and majority (78 per cent) felt the day as very fearful. In I. Polavaram mandal, out of 131 respondents, 3 per cent felt moderate and 97 per cent felt it very fearful. In Ainavilli mandal, out of 163 respondents, 13 per cent felt the day moderate, and majority (87 per cent) felt the day as very fearful. In Katrenikona mandal, out of 143 respondents, 3 per cent felt the day as moderate, 16 per cent fearful and majority (81 per cent) as very fearful. On the whole, out of 600 respondents, majority (85 per cent) felt that their psychological conditions are very fearful and only minority felt moderate and fearful.

Position after Cyclone-Psychological Conditions

The respondents, who witnessed the killer cyclone cannot forget the trauma they and their belongings were subjected to. The psychological status of the respondents after the cyclone is presented in Table-4.14.

Table 4.14: Position after Cyclone-[Psychological Conditions].

Mandal	*Miserable*	*Unhappy*	*Normal*	*Total Respondents*
Amalapuram	23(27.1)	11(12.9)	51(60.0)	85(100.0)
Ambajipeta	23(29.5)	15(19.2)	40(51.3)	78(100.0)
I. Polavaram	35(26.7)	3(2.3)	93(71.0)	131(100.0)
Ainavilli	10(6.2)	2(1.2)	151(92.6)	163(100.0)
Katrenikona	0(0.0)	4(2.8)	139(97.2)	143(100.0)
Total	**91(15.2)**	**35(5.8)**	**474(79.0)**	**600(100.0)**

(Figures in parentheses indicate percentages)

In Amalapuram mandal, out of 85 respondents, 27 per cent told that their condition was miserable, 13 per cent felt it unhappy and 60 per cent enjoyed it in a normal way of life after the cyclone. In Ambajipeta mandal, out of 78 respondents, 30 per cent told that their condition was miserable, 19 per cent are unhappy and half of the respondents are normal. In I. Polavaram mandal, out of 131 respondents, 27 per cent felt miserable, 2 per cent felt unhappy and majority (71 per cent) felt normal. In Ainavilli mandal, out of 163 respondents, 6 per cent are feeling miserable, one per cent feeling unhappy and 93 per cent feeling normal. In Katrenikona mandal, 3 percent are feeling unhappy and majority (97 per cent) are feeling normal.

Overall, out of 600 respondents, 15 per cent told that their psychological conditions were miserable; 6 per cent told that they are unhappy and 79 per cent are accustomed to it as a normal way of life. The above data show that a significant number (15 per cent) are still facing the psychological trauma of the day and significant numbers in Amalapuram, Ambajipeta and I. Polavaram mandals are still experiencing that miserable day.

Position after Cyclone-Opinions about Cyclone

The respondents were asked for their opinions about the cyclone which are presented in Table-4.15:

Table 4.15: Position after Cyclone-[Opinion about Cyclone].

Mandal	*Curse*	*Natural thing*	*Nothing can be done*	*Can be managed to a certain extent*	*Total Respondents*
Amalapuram	51(60.0)	15(17.6)	13(15.3)	6(7.1)	85(100.0)
Ambajipeta	63(80.8)	5(6.4)	7(9.0)	3(3.8)	78(100.0)
I. Polavaram	24(18.3)	31(23.7)	64(48.9)	12(9.1)	131(100.0)
Ainavilli	28(17.2)	77(47.2)	41(25.2)	17(10.4)	163(100.0)
Katrenikona	25(17.5)	17(11.9)	100(69.9)	1(0.7)	143(100.0)
Total	**191(31.8)**	**145(24.2)**	**225(37.5)**	**39(6.5)**	**600(100.0)**

(Figures in parentheses indicate percentages)

Table-4.15 presents the data with regard to the opinions of the respondents about the cyclone. In Amalapuram mandal, out of 85 respondents, majority (60 per cent) opined that it is a curse, 18 per cent opined that it is a natural thing, 15 per cent opined that nothing can be done and only 7 per cent opined that it can be managed to a certain extent. In Ambajipeta mandal, out of 78 respondents, majority (81 per cent) felt that it is a curse and only minority felt that it is a natural thing and nothing can be done and it can be managed to a certain extent. In I. Polavaram mandal, out of 131 respondents, 18 per cent felt the cyclone is a curse, 24 per cent opined that it is a natural thing, 49 per cent opined that nothing can be done and 9 per cent felt that it can be managed to a certain extent. In Ainavilli mandal, out of 163 respondents, 17 per cent told that it is a curse, majority (47 per cent) told that it is a natural thing, 25 per cent felt that nothing can be done and 10 per cent opined that it can be managed to a certain extent. In Katrenikona mandal, out of 143 respondents, 18 per cent opined that it is a curse, 12 per cent told that it is a natural thing, and majority (70 per cent) told that nothing can be done.

On the whole, out of 600 respondents, 32 per cent told that cyclone is a curse, 24 per cent told that it is a natural thing, 38 per cent told that nothing can be done and only 7 per cent opined that it can be managed to a certain extent. Out of the four alternatives, one can be managed to a certain extent which is a wise opinion. Relatively more respondents in I. Polavaram mandal and Ainavilli mandal gave the wise opinion about the cyclone. The answer that is 'curse' shows the innocence of the respondents. Cyclone is a 'natural thing' is also a wise answer and again Ainavilli mandal topped with this answer. The ignorant percentage is more in Ambajipeta and innocent percentage is more in Katrenikona. Overall, relatively the respondents in Ainavilli mandal gave the wise answer.

Part-C

Rescue Received during the Cyclone

The respondents were questioned about the rescue teams during the cyclone. The notification of the Collector, East Godavari District mentioned about the immediate rescue operations during the cyclone.

Table 4.16: Rescue received during the Cyclone.

Mandal	*Central Govt.*	*State Govt.*	*Voluntary Organi-zations*	*Kith-kin*	*Others*	*Total Respon-dents*
Amalapuram	0(0.0)	64(75.3)	0(0.0)	13(15.3)	8(9.4)	85(100.0)
Ambajipeta	0(0.0)	69(88.5)	0(0.0)	2(2.6)	7(8.9)	78(100.0)
I. Polavaram	0(0.0)	49(37.4)	1(0.8)	73(55.7)	8(6.1)	131(100.0)
Ainavilli	0(0.0)	37(22.7)	16(9.8)	86(52.8)	24(14.7)	163(100.0)
Katrenikona	0(0.0)	137(95.8)	2(1.4)	0(0.0)	4(2.8)	143(100.0)
Total	**0(0.0)**	**356(59.3)**	**19(3.2)**	**174(29.0)**	**51(8.5)**	**600(100.0)**

(Figures in parentheses indicate percentages)

Table-4.16 presents the data about the rescue teams that operated in the affected areas during the cyclone. In Amalapuram mandal, out of 85 respondents, majority (75 per cent) told that State government came to their rescue;

15 per cent told that kith and kin came to their rescue and 9 per cent told that others came to their rescue during the cyclone.

In Ambajipeta mandal, out of 78 respondents, 89 per cent told that the State Government came to their rescue; 3 per cent told that kith and kin came to their rescue and 9 per cent told that others came to their rescue during the cyclone.

In I. Polavaram mandal, out of 131 respondents, 37 per cent told that the State Government came to their rescue, while more than half of it told that their kith and kin came to their rescue, 6 per cent told that others came to their rescue and only one per cent told that voluntary organizations came to their rescue during the cyclone.

In Ainavilli mandal, out of 163 respondents, 23 per cent told that the State Government came to their rescue, while 10 per cent told that voluntary organizations came to their rescue, and majority (53 per cent) told that kith and kin came to their rescue and 15 per cent told that others came to their rescue during the cyclone.

In Katrenikona mandal, out of 143 respondents, majority (96 per cent) told that the State Government came to their rescue, and only very few told that voluntary organizations (1 per cent) came to their rescue and 3 per cent told that other came to their rescue during the cyclone.

On the whole, majority (59 per cent) of the respondents told that they received help from the State Government during the cyclone, while only 3 per cent told that they received help from the voluntary organizations. Some respondents (29 per cent) told that they received help from their kith and kin. And 8.5 per cent told that others came to their rescue during the cyclone. It can be seen from the above data that only State Government took active and immediate steps as per the opinions of the majority of respondents besides kith and kin.

Distribution of rice during the period of cyclone damage

Distribution of rice up to some period after damage of cyclone

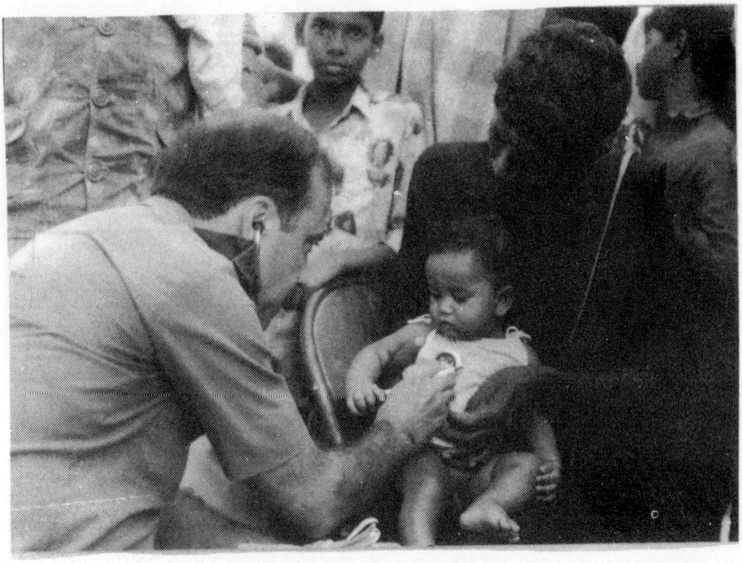

A protected male child being tested by the doctor after his parents being drowned in the flood

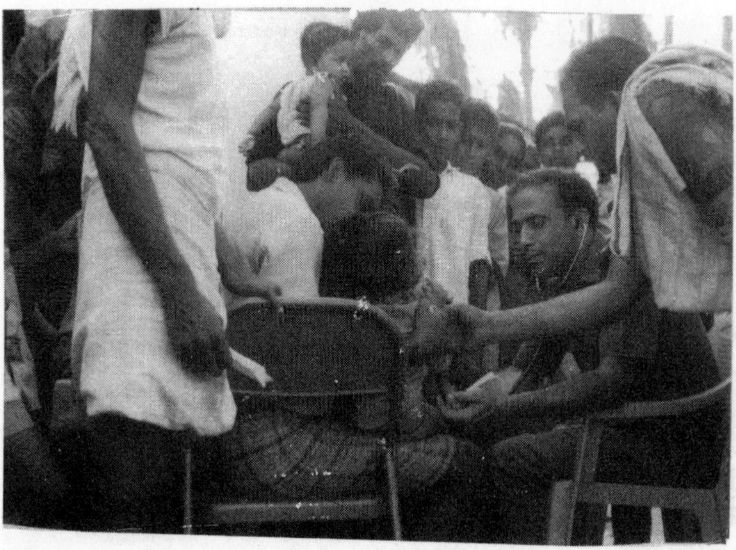

Little ones being tested by the doctor during the pestilence caused by the rubbish things during the cyclone

Kerosene being supplied to the cyclone-hit people

Kerosene being supplied even after cyclone to the victms of cyclone

Rescue Received after the Cyclone

Table-4.17 presents the data with regard to the rescue operations after the cyclone:

Table 4.17: Rescue received after the Cyclone.

Mandal	*Central Govt.*	*State Govt.*	*Voluntary Organizations*	*Kith-kin*	*Others*	*Total Respondents*
Amalapuram	0(0.0)	73(85.9)	1(1.2)	4(4.7)	7(8.2)	85(100.0)
Ambajipeta	0(0.0)	70(89.7)	1(1.3)	2(2.6)	5(6.4)	78(100.0)
I. Polavaram	1(0.8)	92(70.2)	2(1.5)	30(22.9)	6(4.6)	131(100.0)
Ainavilli	1(0.6)	79(48.5)	51(31.3)	19(11.7)	13(7.9)	163(100.0)
Katrenikona	20(13.9)	3(2.2)	118(82.5)	0(0.0)	2(1.4)	143(100.0)
Total	**20(3.2)**	**317(52.8)**	**173(28.8)**	**55(9.2)**	**33(6.0)**	**600(100.0)**

(Figures in parentheses indicate percentages)

In Amalapuram mandal, out of 85 respondents, majority (86 per cent) told that the State Government came to their rescue after the cyclone. Only one per cent told that voluntary organizations came to their rescue, 5 per cent told that kith and kin came to their rescue and 8 per cent told that others came to their rescue.

In Ambajipeta mandal, that out of 78 respondents, majority (90 per cent) told that the State Government came to their rescue; one per cent told that voluntary organizations came to their rescue, 3 per cent told that their kith and kin came to their rescue, and 6 per cent told that others came to their rescue.

In I. Polavaram mandal, that out of 131 respondents, less than one per cent told that the Central Government came to their rescue, majority (70 per cent) told that the State Government came to their rescue, while 2 per cent told that voluntary organizations came to their rescue, significantly, 23 per cent told that their kith and kin came to their rescue, and 5 per cent told that others came to help them after the cyclone.

In Ainavilli mandal, out of 163 respondents, less than one per cent told that the Central Government helped a lot, 31 per cent told that voluntary organizations played an active part in the rescue operations, 12 per cent told that their kith and kin came to their rescue and 8 per cent told that others came to their rescue.

In Katrenikona mandal, that out of 143 respondents, 14 per cent told that the Central Government came to their rescue; 2 per cent told that the State Government came to their rescue, majority (83 per cent) told that voluntary organizations came to their rescue and one per cent told that others came to their rescue.

On the whole, out of 600 respondents, only 3 per cent opined that they received help from the Central Government, while a little more than half told that they received help more from the State Government, and a significant number (29 per cent) told that they received help more from voluntary organizations, 9 per cent told that their kith and kin helped them more than the authorities and 6 per cent told that others came to their rescue more than the authorities. The overall picture shows that half of the respondents are satisfied with the rescue operations of the State Government, while voluntary organizations actively worked in the severely affected mandals, particularly Ainavilli and Katrenikona.

Note:-Respondents were rescued by more than one of the above categories, but the answers were taken for the best rescue operations in the opinions of respondents. It seems that particularly in Katrenikona, the efforts and service of the voluntary organizations is memorable according to the respondents.

Nature of Help Received

After the cyclone, the respondents were given medicines, food grains, kerosene, clothes, money and other necessary items. The distribution of data with regard to the nature of help after cyclone is presented in Table-4.18.

Table 4.18: Nature of help received.

Mandal	*Medicines*	*Food*	*Kerosene*	*Clothes*	*Money*	*Others*
Amalapuram	8(10.8)	3(3.2)	3(3.4)	6(5.0)	79(13.7)	0(0.0)
Ambajipeta	0(0.0)	1(1.1)	1(1.1)	1(0.8)	74(12.9)	0(0.0)
I. Polavaram	2(2.7)	4(4.3)	3(3.4)	24(19.0)	128(22.3)	51(34.0)
Ainavilli	1(1.4)	6(6.4)	6(6.8)	8(6.2)	153(26.6)	66(44.0)
Katrenikona	63(85.1)	80(85.0)	75(85.3)	87(69.0)	141(24.5)	33(22.0)
Total	**74(100.0)**	**94(100.0)**	**88(100.0)**	**126(100.0)**	**575(100.0)**	**150(100.0)**

(Figures in parentheses indicate percentages)

Out of the total 74 respondents who told that they received medicines, 11 percent are in Amalapuram mandal, 3 per cent are in I. Polavaram mandal, one per cent are in Ainavilli mandal and majority (85 per cent) are in Katrenikona mandal.

Out of the total 94 respondents who told that they received food grains, 3 percent are in Amalapuram mandal, 1 per cent are in Ambajipeta mandal, 4 per cent are in I. Polavaram mandal, 6 per cent are in Ainavilli mandal and majority (85 per cent) are in Katrenikona mandal.

Out of the total 88 respondents, who told that they received kerosene, 3 per cent are in Amalapuram mandal, one per cent are in Ambajipeta mandal, 3 per cent are in I. Polavaram mandal, 7 per cent are in Ainavilli mandal and majority (85 per cent) are in Katrenikona mandal.

Out of the total 126 respondents who told that they received clothes, 5 percent are in Amalapuram mandal, one per cent are in Ambajipeta mandal, 19 per cent are in I. Polavaram mandal, 6 per cent are in Ainavilli mandal and majority (69 per cent) are in Katrenikona mandal.

Out of the total 575 respondents who told that they received money, 14 per cent are in Amalapuram mandal,

13 per cent are in Ambajipeta mandal, 22 per cent are in I. Polavaram mandal, 27 per cent are in Ainavilli mandal and 25 per cent are in Katrenikona mandal.

Out of the total 150 respondents who told that they received other necessary items, 34 per cent are in I. Polavaram mandal, 44 per cent are in Ainavilli mandal and 22 per cent are in Katrenikona mandal.

The overall picture of the nature of help received by the respondents shows that 96 per cent of the total sample (600) received the aid ranging from Rs.700-2300 and more, 21 per cent of the total sample received clothes, 15 per cent of the total sample received kerosene, 16 per cent of the total sample received rice, 12 per cent of the total sample received medicines and 25 per cent of the total sample received other necessary items. On the whole, Katrenikona mandal received the maximum help from all the sources when compared to other mandals.

Opinions on Adequacy of Rescue operations

Table-4.19 presents the data with regard to adequacy of rehabilitation programmes: -

Table 4.19: Opinions on Adequacy of Rehabilitation.

Mandal	*Yes*	*No*	*Total Respondents*
Amalapuram	45(52.9)	40(47.1)	85
Ambajipeta	34(43.6)	44(56.4)	78
I. Polavaram	101(77.1)	30(22.9)	131
Ainavilli	75(46.0)	88(54.0)	163
Katrenikona	135(94.4)	8(5.6)	143
Total	**390(65.0)**	**210(35.0)**	**600(100.0)**

(Figures in parentheses indicate percentages)

In Amalapuram mandal, out of 85 respondents, 53 per cent are satisfied with the rehabilitation programmes after the cyclone, whereas 47 per cent are dissatisfied with the programmes. In Ambajipeta mandal, out of 78 respondents, 44 per cent are satisfied and 56 per cent are dissatisfied. In I. Polavaram mandal, out of 131 respondents, majority (77 per cent) are satisfied and 23 per cent are dissatisfied. In Ainavilli mandal, out of 163 respondents, 46 per cent are satisfied and 54 per cent are dissatisfied. In Katrenikona mandal, out of 143 respondents, majority (94 per cent) are satisfied, and only 6 per cent are dissatisfied with the programmes.

On the whole, out of 600 respondents, 65 per cent are satisfied with the rehabilitation programmes, whereas 35 per cent are dissatisfied with the programmes. It shows that two-thirds of the respondents are satisfied with the rehabilitation programmes.

Opinions on Deficiencies of Rehabilitation

The respondents were asked about the deficiencies of rehabilitation programmes with various alternatives viz., insufficient funds, undue delay, lack of commitment, lack of co-ordination, emergence of corruption and any other favourtism.

Table 4.20: Opinion on deficiencies of Rehabilitation

A. Insufficient Funds; B. Undue delay; C. Lack of Commitment; D. Lack of Co-ordination; E. Corruption; F. Any other favouritism.

Mandal	*Insufficient Funds*	*Undue delay*	*Lock of Commitment*	*Lack of Co-ordination*	*Corruption*	*Any other favouritsm*
Amalapuram	70(13.4)	27(14.6)	22(35.5)	22(26.8)	4(7.5)	0(0.0)
Ambajipeta	59(11.3)	26(14.1)	25(40.3)	43(52.4)	10(18.9)	3(37.5)
I. Polavaram	107(20.5)	39(21.1)	3(4.8)	2(2.4)	7(13.2)	1(12.5)
Ainavilli	147(28.1)	45(24.3)	12(19.4)	14(17.1)	31(58.5)	2(25.0)
Katrenikona	138(26.4)	48(25.9)	0(0.0)	1(1.2)	1(1.9)	2(25.0)
Total	**523(87.2)**	**185(30.8)**	**62(10.3)**	**82(13.7)**	**53(8.8)**	**8(1.3)**

(Figures in parentheses indicate percentages)

Table-4.20 presents the data of opinions on deficiencies of Rehabilitation. Out of the total 523 respondents who answered that funds are insufficient, 13 per cent are in Amalapuram mandal, 11 per cent are in Ambajipeta mandal, 21 per cent are in I. Polavaram mandal, 28 per cent are in Ainavilli mandal and 26 per cent are in Katrenikona mandal.

Out of the total 185 respondents who opined that there is undue delay in the rehabilitation programmes, 15 per cent are in Amalapuram mandal, 14 per cent are in Ambajipeta mandal, 21 per cent are in I. Polavaram mandal, 24 per cent are in Ainavilli mandal and 26 per cent are in Katrenikona mandal.

Out of the total 62 respondents who told that there is lack of commitment among the assigned officials, 36 per cent are in Amalapuram mandal, 40 per cent are in Ambajipeta mandal, 5 per cent are in I. Polavaram mandal, and 19 per cent are in Ainavilli mandal.

Out of the total 82 respondents who told that there is lack of co-ordination, 27 per cent are in Amalapuram mandal, 52 per cent are in Ambajipeta mandal, 2 per cent are in I. Polavaram mandal, 17 per cent are in Ainavilli mandal and only one per cent are in Katrenikona mandal.

Out of the total 53 respondents who told that the officials are corrupt, 8 per cent are in Amalapuram mandal, 19 per cent are in Ambajipeta mandal, 13 per cent are in I. Polavaram mandal, 56 per cent are in Ainavilli mandal and only 2 per cent are in Katrenikona mandal.

Out of the total 8 respondents who opined that favourtism took place in the rehabilitation operations, 38 per cent are in Ambajipeta mandal, 13 per cent are in I. Polavaram mandal, 25 per cent each in Ainavilli mandal and Katrenikona mandals.

On the whole, the total picture shows that among the total 600 respondents, majority (87 per cent) opined that insufficient funds are one of the main deficiencies of the rehabilitation programmes. Among the total, 31 per cent opined that undue delay took place in the rehabilitation programmes, 10 per cent told that there is lack of commitment among the officials and that there is no service-bent of mind, and only for name-sake they did the programmes, another 14 per cent told that there is lack of co-ordination among the Central Govt., State Govt., and voluntary organizations. All concentrated only in few totally affected areas and neglected others. A few (9 per cent) opined that corruption also took place in these programmes, and only one per cent told that favourism took place. It is noticeable that insufficient funds are the main reason for the dissatisfaction among the respondents while significant number of respondents felt that delay occurred in implementing rehabilitation programmes.

Opinions on Rehabilitation Facilities

The respondents were asked about their opinions on the Rehabilitation facilities. The given alternatives are: very happy, happy, satisfactory, unhappy and very unhappy.

Table 4.21: Opinions on Rehabilitation facilities.

Mandal	*Very Happy*	*Happy*	*Satis-factory*	*Unhappy*	*Very unhappy*	*Total Respondents*
Amalapuram	8(9.4)	27(31.8)	12(14.1)	28(32.9)	10(11.8)	85(100.00
Ambajipeta	4(5.1)	29(37.2)	4(5.1)	22(28.2)	19(24.4)	78(100.0)
I. Polavaram	1(0.8)	91(69.5)	10(7.6)	26(19.8)	3(2.3)	131(100.0)
Ainavilli	5(3.1)	75(46.0)	8(4.9)	66(40.5)	9(5.5)	163(100.0)
Katrenikona	1(0.7)	122(85.3)	10(7.0)	4(2.8)	6(4.2)	143(100.0)
Total	**19(3.3)**	**344(57.3)**	**44(7.3)**	**146(24.3)**	**47(7.8)**	**600(100.0)**

(Figures in parentheses indicate percentages)

The distribution of the data based on the respondents' opinions on rehabilitation facilities is presented in Table-4.21. In Amalapuram mandal, out of 85 respondents, 9 per cent felt very happy, 32 per cent happy, 14 per cent satisfied, 33 per cent unhappy and 12 percent much unhappy with the rehabilitation facilities.

In Ambajipeta mandal out of 78 respondents, 5 per cent are very happy with the rehabilitation facilities, 37 per cent are just happy, 5 per cent are satisfied, 28 per cent are not happy and 24 percent are very much unhappy, with the rehabilitation facilities.

In I. Polavaram mandal out of 131 respondents less than one per cent felt very happy, majority (70 per cent) felt happy, 8 per cent are satisfied, 20 per cent are unhappy and 2 per cent felt very unhappy with the rehabilitation facilities.

In Ainavilli mandal out of 163 respondents, only 3 per cent are very happy, 46 per cent are happy, 5 per cent are satisfied, 41 per cent are unhappy and 6 percent expressed very unhappy regarding the facilities.

In Katrenikona mandal out of 143 respondents less than one per cent are very happy, majority (85 per cent) expressed happiness, 7 per cent are satisfied, 3 per cent are unhappy and another 4 per cent have very much expressed their unhappiness regarding the facilities.

On the whole, out of the total 600 respondents only 3 per cent expressed their extreme happiness, majority (57 per cent) felt happy and 7 per cent are satisfied with the programmes. Whereas the respondents who expressed unhappiness are 24 per cent and unhappiest respondents are 8 per cent. Overall, 11 per cent are in extreme categories and 7 per cent are in between. Nearly one-fourth of the respondents expressed dissatisfaction about the programmes, and majority (57 per cent) expressed satisfaction, regarding the rehabilitation programmes.

Relatively more number of respondents in Amalapuram mandal felt very happy (9 per cent) and more number of respondents in Ambajipeta mandal (24 per cent) felt very unhappy. Relatively more number of respondents felt happy in Katrenikona mandal with 85 per cent and the number of respondents in Ainavilli (41 per cent) felt unhappy, with the programmes. The satisfied percentage is more in Amalapuram mandal with 14 per cent, than in other mandals.

While summarizing the data in Part-A, which deals with the extent of damage to lives and property, the following observations are made by the researcher. The sample denotes that 166 deaths occurred on the whole and majority of deaths (94 cases) were reported in I. Polavaram mandal, followed by Katrenikona mandal and Ainavilli mandal. The extent of damage to property in the selected mandals is Rs.35,705,870. As a matter of fact, the extent of damage to landed property is more (54 per cent) as the area is famous for coconuts and paddy, followed by 42 per cent damage to residential houses and 4 per cent damage to livestock. While taking the statistics of damage to crops in particular, coconut plants are badly affected with 56 per cent damage, followed by 35 per cent damage to paddy with Vegetables and Banana crops also being affected in these areas.

While coming to Part-B, the summary of restoration position of respondents as observed by the researcher is, that on the whole, 71.5 per cent of the total sample told that they are restored to their original position, and 28.5 per cent told they are not yet restored. Majority (45 per cent) took 3-6 months period to restore and 37 per cent of respondents took one to two years and even more to restore themselves from the cyclone devastation. Majority of the respondents (34 per cent) spent Rs.10,000-20,000 to repair damages towards property, and a significant percentage (15 per cent) spent Rs.50,000 and more. A little more than half of the respondents spent less than Rs.10,000 from their won finances towards restoration. Nearly half of the respondents spent less than Rs.10,000 from the sources of loan. Half of the respondents spent Rs.10,000-20,000 towards restoration from the above two sources. All the respondents got aid from the authorities, but the amount varies from respondent to respondent, depending upon the extent of damage. But all the Central, State Government, along with the voluntary organizations concentrated on the severely affected areas and poured funds accordingly. This is also one of the reasons for the variations of aid. Anyhow, majority (37 per cent) of the respondents got aid worth Rs.700-1100 and 14 per cent got the highest amount which happened to be in the severely affected mandals wherein more deaths took place.

The respondents' opinions about the productivity of crops show that half of the respondents are partly satisfied and 30 per cent are dissatisfied with the yields of their crops after the cyclone. After the cyclone, a little more than half of the respondents felt the scarcity of money. The respondents also felt the scarcity of food, clothing, water, medicines and other necessary items after the cyclone. Nearly half of the respondents felt that the living conditions are very bad after the cyclone. Majority of the respondents (85 per cent) expressed that their psychological conditions are very fearful during the cyclone and even after the cyclone. A significant number (15 per cent) expressed that still the miserable experiences of that day are haunting their minds. Most of the respondents (38 per cent) opined that nothing can be done about the cyclone followed by the opinions like cyclone is a curse and that it is a natural thing. Only a minority (7 per cent) opined that it can be managed to a certain extent.

Part-C deals with rescue and rehabilitation programmes. Majority of the respondents (59 per cent) felt that the State Government came to their rescue during the cyclone. A significant number (29 per cent) of the total sample opined that their close relatives came to their rescue during the cyclone, which shows that majority of the people in the affected areas did not get immediate help from the authorities, and it might be one of the reasons for their dissatisfaction with regard to rescue operations.

A little more than half of the respondents expressed their satisfaction with regard to the rescue operations of the State Government, and followed by the efforts of the voluntary organizations after the cyclone. Especially, in the selected mandals like Katrenikona and Ainavilli, services and money were provided by the voluntary organizations, which is really laudable, in the words of respondents. All the respondents received monetary help from the authorities after the cyclone though the amount varies from mandal to mandal because of lack of coordination among the officials and voluntary organizations. Majority of respondents did not get the necessary items like medicines, food grains, kerosene, clothes etc., after the cyclone. Even the then R.D.O. of Amalapuram Revenue Division also expressed his inability in providing food, drinking water, accommodation and shelter because the relief camps were flooded with people with more than their capacity with the total devastation of the entire area. In Amalapuram Revenue Division 333 relief camps were organized for a total number of 1,33,702 evacuees. Majority (65 per cent) of the respondents opined that the rescue operations are adequate whereas 35 per cent told that they experienced with inadequate rescue operations. Majority of the respondents (87 per cent) cited that funds are insufficient, 31 per cent felt that there was undue delay in the rehabilitation facilities and others cited reasons for the deficiencies of Rehabilitation as due to lack of commitment among the officials and lack of co-ordination among the Central and State Government and voluntary organizations and there were traces of corruption and favouritism among the officials. On the whole, a little more than half of the respondents expressed their happiness towards the rehabilitation facilities.

5

Discussion

Restoration and Rehabilitation are the most important key variables in the study of natural disasters which occur too infrequently to warrant (or force) a great expenditure of money, attention or managerial expertise. On the whole, it seems that many governments are not in fact capable of providing an efficient response to a natural disaster any more than they can ameliorate or prevent man-made disaster, or deliver basic services (health, shelter, food) to their populations (Stephen, P. Cohen & C.V. Raghavulu, 1979). Information-prior to during and subsequent to a disater-is itself a major variable. Many "victims" would not die or suffer if they had perfect information about an impending event, but such information may be technically impossible to acquire. The cyclones are predictable in terms of general probability, but widely unpredictable in terms of either specific time or place of occurrence. Thus, these resemble the strategic bombing campaigns of World War II in each case preparation for attack may save a good percentage of population, but it is unlikely to save all. It is a doubtful question whether to concentrate on ameliorative measures like cyclone-proof constructions, cyclone-relief centers etc., (since there are chances of a particular protected area may be bypassed and chances of direct attack by an unprotected area or areas). So, limited preparations against a cyclone may be ineffective, if the disaster occurs elsewhere, and the most elaborate are likely to fail in the face of a storm surge.

Further, a natural disaster has a selective social impact upon a victim population. The natural disasters like cyclones, famines and floods are likely to kill poor people while the rich can afford to buy food or leave the affected area. In this context, Cohen & Raghavulu (1979) say that "Societies generally assign greater culpability in the sense that the inequalities of society if ignored by the State and relief workers imply the death of some and the escape of others. Besides, the poor elderly women and children are the victims to natural disasters than males.

The restoration of the affected people depends upon how best the authorities provide rescue and rehabilitation programmes besides individual effort. Eavacuation or rescue in the case of cyclones requires near-perfect information as well as an efficient system of population movement to safer places or relief camps. The then Revenue Divisional Officer, Amalapuram opines that at the time of cyclone evacuation of people became difficult because the physiogeographic, adalphic, water morphology conditions are not convenient for easy evacuation. Owing to the existence of island mandals and island villages and also lack of proper transportation and communication, there is a communication gap between higher and lower level administration and village level administration i.e., from Collector to Village Administrative Officer (V.A.O). e.g. the V.A.O. who was on the mission to disseminate cyclone message to Balusutippa was held up on the way due to high tides and in turn he brought the same to the notice of mandal level machinery after one and a half days. This led for not taking immediate evacuation. All these factors had its impact on the restoration of the affected people. In this context, respondent's caste, age, literacy level, occupation and household income are taken for analysis and presented through cross-tables in two Sections.

Part-A

Caste-wise Restoration

Among the total sample of 600, the restored respondents are 429 and 171 respondents are not yet restored. In Table-5.1, caste-wise restoration of the respondents is given (see at the end of the Chapter-V).

In the Table-5.1 two variables are analysed for study. They are: Restoration and Caste. The variable 'Restoration' has two sub-variables 'restored and not restored'. The mandal-wise data of restoration with regard to caste is as follows:

In Amalapuram mandal, out of 85 respondents, 45 are restored and 40 are not restored. Out of 45 restored respondents, 33 per cent belonged to forward castes while majority (62 per cent) belonged to Backward Castes and only a small minority (4 per cent) belonged to Scheduled Castes. Out of 40, not-restored respondents, 48 per cent and 45 per cent belonged to Forward Castes, and to Backward Castes respectively, while the remaining related to Scheduled Castes.

In Ambajipeta mandal, out of the total 78 respondents, only 20 are restored and majority (58) are not-restored. Out of the 20 restored respondents, 45 per cent belonged to Forward Castes, 5 per cent belonged to Backward Castes, and half of the respondents (50 per cent) belonged to Scheduled Castes. Out of the 58 not restored respondents, majority (41 per cent) belonged to Forward Castes, 19 per cent belonged to Backward Castes, 28 per cent belonged to Scheduled Castes and 12 per cent belonged to Scheduled Tribes.

In I. Polavaram mandal, out of 131 respondents, majority (126) are restored and only 5 are not restored. Out of the 126 restored respondents, 47 per cent belonged to Forward Castes, 40 per cent belonged to Backward

Table 5.1: Caste-wise Restoration.

Mandal	*Restored*					*Not-restored*					*Grand*
	F.C.	*B.C.*	*S.C.*	*S.T.*	*Total Restored*	*F.C.*	*B.C.*	*S.C.*	*S.T.*	*Total Not-restored*	*Total*
Amalapuram	15 (33.3) (10.3)	28 (62.3) (18.4)	2 (4.4) (1.5)	0 (0.0) (0.0)	45 (100.0) (10.5)	19 (47.5) (32.8)	18 (45.0) (24.3)	3 (7.5) (9.4)	0 (0.0) (0.0)	40 (100.0) (23.4)	85
Ambajipeta	9 (45.0) (6.2)	1 (5.0) (0.7)	10 (50.0) (7.6)	0 (0.00 (0.0)	20 (100.0) (4.7)	24 (41.4) (41.4)	11 (18.9) (14.9)	16 (27.6) (50.0)	7 (12.1) (100.0)	58 (100.0) (33.9)	78
I. Polavaram	59 (46.8) (40.7)	50 (39.7) (32.9)	16 (12.7) (12.3)	1 (100.0)	126(100.0) (29.4)	1 (20.0) (1.6)	4 (80.0) (5.4)	0 (0.0) (0.0)	0 (0.0) (0.0)	5 (100.0) (2.9)	131
Ainavilli	45 (29.8) (31.1)	41 (27.2) (27.0)	65 (43.0) (49.6)	0 (0.0) (0.0)	151(100.0) (35.2)	11 (91.7) (19.0)	1 (8.3) (1.4)	0 (0.0) (0.0)	0 (0.0) (0.0)	12 (100.0) (7.0)	163
Katrenikona	17 (19.5) (11.7)	32 (36.8) (21.0)	38 (43.7) (29.0)	0 (0.0) (0.0)	87 (100.0) (20.2)	3 (5.4) (5.2)	40 (71.4) (54.0)	13 (23.2) (40.6)	0 (0.0) (0.0)	56 (100.0) (32.8)	143
Total	**145(33.8) (100.0)**	**152(35.4) (100.0)**	**131(30.5) (100.0)**	**1(0.3) (100.0)**	**429(100.0) (100.0)**	**58(33.9) (100.0)**	**74(43.3) (100.0)**	**32(18.7) (100.0)**	**7(4.1) (100.0)**	**171(100.0) (100.0)**	**600**

(figures in horizontal parentheses indicate percentages with regard to restored and not-restored)
(figures in vertical parentheses indicate percentages with regard to caste)

Castes, 13 per cent belonged to Scheduled Castes and less than one per cent belonged to Scheduled Tribes. Out of the 5 not-restored respondents, 20 per cent belonged to Forward Castes and 80 per cent belonged to Backward Castes.

In Ainavilli mandal, out of 163 respondents, majority (151 respondents) are restored and only 12 are not-restored. Out of the 151 restored respondents, 30 per cent belonged to Forward Castes, 27 per cent belonged to Backward Castes and 43 per cent belonged to Scheduled Castes. Among the 12 not-restored respondents, majority belonged to Forward Castes and only 8 per cent belonged to Backward Castes (87 respondents).

In Katrenikona mandal, out of 143 respondents, 61 per cent are restored and 39 per cent (56 respondents) are not restored. Among the restored respondents, 20 per cent belonged to Forward Castes, 37 per cent belonged to Backward Castes and 44 per cent belonged to Scheduled Castes. Among the 56 not-restored respondents, 5 per cent belonged to Forward Castes, majority (71 per cent) belonged to Backward Castes and 23 per cent belonged to Scheduled Castes.

On the whole, out of 600 respondents, 429 (72 per cent) are restored and 171 (28 per cent) are not-restored. The overall data on the restored respondents show that, one-third of the restored belonged to Forward Castes 35 per cent belonged to Backward Castes, 31 per cent belonged to Scheduled Castes and only one respondent belonged to Scheduled Tribes. Among the not-restored respondents (171), one-third belonged to Forward Castes, 43 per cent belonged to Backward Castes, 19 per cent belonged to Scheduled Castes and only 4 percent belonged to Scheduled Tribes.

The following observations may be made basing upon the caste-wise analysis of the respondents:

There are differences from mandal to mandal, with regard to restoration, even though majority 429 (71.5 per cent) are restored in the total sample.

1. In Amalapuram mandal, the restored and not-restored are almost equal in size (with 53 per cent and 47 per cent).

   In Ambajipeta mandal, majority (74 per cent) are not-restored. In I. Polavaram mandal (96 per cent) and in Ainavilli mandal (93 per cent) are restored. In Katrenikona mandal, 61 per cent are restored and 39 per cent are not-restored. That means, in terms of restoration, I. Polavaram, Ainavilli, Katrenikona and Amalapuram mandals come first, second, third and fourth positions respectively and only in Ambajipeta majority are not-restored [Refer Table-5.11(a)].

2.

   (a) As we notified mandal-wise differences, we also notified caste-wise differences in terms of restoration. While looking from the caste angle, out of the 429 (71.5 per cent) restored respondents, 35 per cent are of the Backward Castes respondents are restored, followed by Forward Castes (34 per cent) and Scheduled Castes (31 per cent). The Backward Caste restored respondents (33 per cent) are more in I. Polavaram mandal. The Forward Caste restored respondents (42 per cent) are also more in I. Polavaram mandal while the Scheduled Caste restored respondents (50 per cent) are more in Ainavilli mandal, with the corresponding restored respondents in the respective mandals [Refer Table-5.1 (a)].

   (b) Among the not-restored respondents, Ambajipeta mandal comes first with 74 per cent followed by Amalapuram mandal with

47 per cent and Katrenikona mandal with 39 per cent. In Ainavilli and I. Polavaram mandals only a few are not-restored [Refer Table-5.1 (a)].

Table 5.1 (a): Mandal-wise Restoration.

Mandal	*Restored*	*Not-restored*	*Total*
Amalapuram	45 (52.9)	40 (47.1)	85 (100.0)
Ambajipeta	20 (25.6)	58 (74.4)	78 (100.0)
I. Polavaram	126 (96.2)	5 (3.8)	131 (100.0)
Ainavilli	151 (92.6)	12 (7.4)	163 (100.0)
Katrenikona	87 (60.8)	56 (39.2)	143 (100.0)
Total	**429 (71.5)**	**171 (28.5)**	**600 (100.0)**

Table-5.1 (b): Caste-wise Restoration

Mandal	*Restored*	*Not-restored*	*Total*
Forward caste	145 (24.2)	58 (9.6)	203 (33.8)
Backward Caste	152 (25.3)	74 (12.4)	226 (37.7)
Scheduled Caste	131 (21.8)	32 (5.4)	163 (27.2)
Scheduled Tribe	1 (0.1)	7 (1.2)	8 (1.3)
Total	**429 (71.5)**	**171 (28.5)**	**600 (100.0)**

(c) Among the not-restored respondents (28.5 per cent) 43 per cent belonged to Backward Castes, followed by Forward Castes (34 per cent), Scheduled Castes (19 per cent) and a small minority (4 per cent) of Scheduled Tribes. Among the not-restored Backward Caste respondents, majority (54 per cent) are in Katrenikona mandal, while majority of Forward Caste not-restored respondents (41 per cent) are in Ambajipeta mandal mandal and majority of Scheduled Caste and Scheduled Tribe not-restored respondents are also more in Ambajipeta (50 per cent and 100 per cent) [Refer-Table-1(a)].

3. Out of the 600 respondents, majority are restored (71.5 per cent) and only 28.5 per cent are not-restored:

   (a) Out of 600 more number of restored (25 per cent) belonged to Backward Castes, followed by Forward Castes (24 per cent) and Scheduled Castes (22 per cent).

   (b) More number of not-restored respondents also belong to Backward Castes (12 per cent), followed by Forward Castes (10 per cent) and 5 per cent in case of Scheduled Castes.

   (c) On the whole also, Backward Caste respondents are more with 38 per cent, followed by 34 per cent Forward Caste respondents and 27 per cent Scheduled Caste respondents.

4. More number of Backward Caste respondents are not-restored, compared to other groups.

Age wise-Restoration

Among the total sample of 600 respondents, the restored are 429 (71.5 per cent) and the not-restored are 171 (28 per cent) In Table-5.2, Age structure vs. restoration is given, [For Table-5.2, 5.2(a) and 5.2 (b)].

In Amalapuram mandal, out of 85 respondents 45 (53 per cent) are restored and 40 (47 per cent) are not-restored [Refer-Table-5.2 (a)]. Out of 45 restored respondents, 4 per cent of them were under 20-29 age-group, 31 per cent under 30-39 age-group, 33 per cent under 40-49 age-group, 14 per cent under 50-59 age-group and only 5 per cent were of 60-69 age-group.

Out of the 40 not-restored respondents 8 per cent belonged to 20-29 age-group, 15 per cent belonged to 30-39 age-group, 37 per cent belonged to 40-49 age-group, 25 per cent belonged to 50-59 age-group and the remaining belonged to 60-69 age-group.

Table 5.2: Age-wise Restoration.

A: [20-29] B:[30-39] C: [40-49] D: [50-59] E: [60-69] F: [70-79]

Mandal	*Restored*						
	A	*B*	*C*	*D*	*E*	*F*	*T*
Amalapuram	2 (4.4) (8.0)	14(31.2) (11.3)	15 (33.3) (11.6)	11 (24.4) (14.1)	3 (6.7) (5.2)	0 (0.0) (0.0)	45 (100.0) (10.5)
Ambajipeta	2 (10.0) (8.0)	5 (25.0) (4.0)	2 (10.0) (1.6)	4 (20.0) (5.1)	7 (35.0) (12.0)	0 (0.0) (0.0)	20 (100.0) (4.7)
I. Polavaram	6 (4.8) (24.0)	52 (41.3) (41.9)	34 (27.0) (26.4)	21 (16.7) (26.9)	11 (8.7) (19.0)	2 (1.5) (13.3)	126 (100.0) (29.4)
Ainavilli	6 (4.0) (24.0)	34 (22.5) (27.4)	48 (31.8) (37.2)	33 (21.9) (42.3)	22 (14.6) (37.9)	8 (5.2) (53.3)	151 (100.0) (35.2)
Katrenikona	9 (10.3) (36.0)	19 (21.8) (15.4)	30 (34.5) (23.2)	9 (10.4) (11.6)	15 (17.3) (25.9)	5 (5.7) (33.3)	87 (100.0) (20.2)
Total	**25(5.8) (100.0)**	**124(28.9) (100.0)**	**129(30.1) (100.0)**	**78 (18.2) (100.0)**	**58(13.5) (100.0)**	**15(3.5) (100.0)**	**429(100.0) (100.0)**

(Table Contd...)

Table 5.2: Contd...

Mandal	*Not-restored*							*Grand*
	A	*B*	*C*	*D*	*E*	*F*	*T*	*Total*
Amalapuram	3 (7.5) (15.8)	6 (15.0) (19.4)	15 (37.5) (29.4)	10 (25.0) (28.6)	6 (15.0) (22.2)	0 (0.0) (0.0)	40 (100.0) (23.4)	85
Ambajipeta	4 (6.9) (21.0)	10 (17.2) (32.3)	14 (24.2) (27.5)	12 (20.7) (34.2)	10 (17.2) (37.0)	8 (13.8) (100.0)	58 (100.0) (33.9)	78
I. Polavaram	0 (0.0) (0.0)	1 (20.0) (3.2)	3 (20.0) (3.2)	1 (20.0) (2.9)	0 (0.0) (0.0)	0 (0.0) (0.0)	5 (100.0) (2.9)	131
Ainavilli	1 (8.3) (5.3)	1 (8.3) (3.2)	7 (58.4) (13.7)	0 (0.0) (0.0)	3 (25.0) (11.2)	0 (0.0) (0.0)	12 (100.0) (7.0)	163
Katrenikona	11 (19.7) (57.9)	13 (23.2) (41.9)	12 (21.4) (23.5)	12 (21.4) (34.3)	8 (14.3) (29.6)	0 (0.0) (0.0)	56 (100.0) (32.8)	143
Total	**19 (11.1) (100.0)**	**31 (18.1) (100.0)**	**51 (29.8) (100.0)**	**35 (20.5) (100.0)**	**27 (15.8) (100.0)**	**8 (4.7) (100.0)**	**71 (100.0) (100.0)**	**600**

(figures in horizontal parentheses indicate percentages with regard to restored and not-restored)
(figures in vertical parentheses indicate percentages with regard to age)

Table 5.2 (a): Mandal-wise Restoration.

Mandal	*Restored*	*Not-restored*	*Total*
Amalapuram	45 (52.9)	40 (47.1)	85 (100.0)
Ambajipeta	20 (25.6)	58 (74.4)	78 (100.0)
I. Polavaram	126 (96.2)	5 (3.8)	131 (100.0)
Ainavilli	151 (92.6)	12 (7.4)	163 (100.0)
Katrenikona	87 (60.8)	56 (39.2)	143 (100.0)
Total	**429 (71.5)**	**171 (28.5)**	**600 (100.0)**

Table 5.2 (b): Age-wise Restoration.

Age	*Restored*	*Not-restored*	*Total*
20-29	25 (4.2)	19 (3.1)	44 (7.3)
30-39	124 (20.7)	31 (5.1)	155 (25.8)
40-49	129 (21.5)	51 (8.5)	180 (30.0)
50-59	78 (13.0)	35 (5.8)	113 (18.8)
60-69	58 (9.7)	27 (4.5)	85 (14.2)
70-79	15 (2.5)	8 (1.4)	23 (3.9)
Total	**429 (71.5)**	**171 (28.5)**	**600 (100.0)**

In Ambajipeta mandal, out of 78 respondents, (26 per cent) a little about one-fourth of them on are restored and the majority (74 per cent) are not-restored. Among the 20 per cent respondents, 10 per cent belonged to 20-29 age-group, 25 per cent belonged to 40-49 age-group, 20 per cent belonged to 50-59 age-group and, significantly, 35 per cent belonged to 60-69 age-group.

Whereas among the 58 not-restored respondents, 7' per cent belonged to 20-29 age-group, 17 per cent belonged to 30-39, 24 per cent belonged to 40-49, 21 per cent belonged to 50-59 age-group, and, significantly, 31 per cent belonged to the highest (60-79) age-group.

In I. Polavaram mandal, out of 131respondents, majority (96 per cent) are restored and a few (4 per cent) are not-restored. Among the 126 restored respondents, 5 per cent belonged to 20-29 age-group, 41 per cent belonged to 30-39 age-group, 27 per cent belonged to 40-49 age-group, 17 per cent belonged to 50-59 age-group while the remaining 10 per cent belonged to the highest (60-79) age-groups.

Among the 5 not-restored respondents, about one-fifth of them belonged to 30-39 age-group, whereas majority (60 per cent) belonged to 40-49 age-group and only 3 per cent belonged to 50-59 age-group.

In Ainavilli mandal out of 163 respondents, majority (93 per cent) are restored and only 7 per cent are not-restored. Among the 151 restored respondents, 4 per cent belonged to 20-29 age-group, 23 per cent belonged to 30-39 age-group, 32 per cent belonged to 40-49 age-group, 22 per cent belonged to 50-59 age-group and, significantly, 19 per cent belonged to the highest (60-79) age-group.

Whereas among the 12 restored respondents, 8 percent each belonged to 20-29 and 30-39 age-groups, majority (58%) belonged to 40-49 age-group and significantly 25 percent belonged to the highest age-group (60-69).

In Katrenikona out of 143 respondents, majority (61 per cent) are restored and 39 per cent are not-restored. Among the restored respondents, 10 per cent belonged to 20-29 age-group, 22 per cent belonged to 30-39 age-group, 35 per cent belonged to 40-49 age-group, 10 per cent belonged to 50-59 age-group and, significantly, 23 per cent belonged to the highest (60-79) age-group.

Whereas among the 56 not-restored respondents, 20 per cent belonged to 20-29 age-group, 23 per cent belonged to 30-39 age-group, 21 per cent each belonged to 40-49 and 50-59 age-groups, and 14 per cent belonged to the highest (60-69) age-group.

The overall scenario shows that among the 429 (71.5 per cent) restored respondents, 6 per cent belonged to 20-

29 age-group, 29 per cent belonged to 30-39 age-group, 30 per cent belonged to 40-49 age-group, 18 per cent belonged to 50-59 age-group and, significantly, 17 per cent belonged to the highest (60-79) age-group.

Out of the 171 (28.5 per cent) not-restored respondents, 11 per cent belonged to 20-29 age-group, 18 per cent belonged to 30-39 age-group, 30 per cent belonged to 40-49 age-group, 20 per cent belonged to 50-59 age-group and, significantly, 21 per cent belonged to the highest (60-79) age-group.

The following observations can be made with regard to age-wise restoration of the respondents:

1. There are differences from mandal to mandal with regard to restorations even though majority (71.5 per cent) are restored in the total sample. As explained in Table-5.2(a), I. Polavaram mandal topped the list with 96 per cent restored respondents followed by Ainavilli mandal (93 per cent), Katrenikona mandal (61 per cent), Amalapuram mandal (53 per cent) and only one-quarter (26 per cent) of respondents in Ambajipeta mandal are restored whereas Ambajipeta mandal topped with 74 per cent not-restored respondents followed by Amalapuram mandal (47 per cent) Katrenikona mandal (39 per cent) and the other two mandals I. Polavaram and Ainavilli only are with small minority of not-restored respondents.

2.

(a) As we noticied mandal-wase differences we also noticied age-wise differences in terms of restoration. While looking through the age-groups among the restored, majority (59 per cent) belong to middle-age-group (30-49) followed by 18 per cent of 50-59 age-group and 17 per cent old-age-group and only 6 per

cent of young age-group. Comparatively the middle-aged respondents are more in I. Polavaram mandal while 50-59 age-groups and old age-group respondents are more in Ainavilli mandal while young age-group respondents are more in Katrenikona mandal (Refer the vertical percentages in Table-5.2).

(b) Hawing a cursory look at the age-groups among the not-restored respondents, 47 per cent belonged to middle-aged (30-49) followed by 21 per cent who belonged to 50-59 age-group and 20 per cent belonged to old-aged. Significantly 11 per cent belonged to younger age-group. Among the not-restored the middle-aged respondents are more in Katrenikona mandal, the old-aged respondents are more in Ambajipeta mandal and the young-aged are more in Katrenikona mandal.

(c) Comparatively the extreme age-group respondents are more in not-restored group than in restored group: -

3. Out of the total 600 sample, majority (71 per cent) are restored and only 28.5 per cent are not-restored.

(a) Out of the total 600, more number of restored respondents are middle-aged (42 per cent) followed by the respondents in the age-group of 50-59 (13 per cent) and old aged (13 per cent)

(b) More number of not-restored respondents are also middle-aged (14 per cent) followed by old-aged respondents (7 per cent) and 6 per cent in 50-59 age-group.

(c) On the whole middle-aged (56 per cent) are in majority in the total sample followed by 19

per cent 50-59 age-group with a significant number 18 per cent old aged respondents.

4.

(*a*) In comparison we can say that more number of restored respondents are middle-aged.

(*b*) More number of young-aged (out of total 44 in the age-group of 20-29) are not-restored.

Literacy Levels-Restoration

Among the total sample of 600, the restored respondents are 4.29 (71.5 per cent) and 171 (28.5 per cent) are not-restored. In the Table-5.3 Literacy-wise restoration is presented (See at the end of the Chapter).

In Amalapuram mandal, out of 85 respondents, more than half of them are restored and 47 per cent are not-restored. Among the restored respondents, 13 per cent are illiterates, 31 per cent studied upto primary, 13 per cent each studied upto upper primary and secondary, 4 per cent studied Inter and 25 per cent have high academic qualifications.

Whereas among the not-restored respondents, 15 per cent are illiterates, 28 per cent studied upto primary, 8 per cent studied upto upper primary, 18 per cent studied upto secondary, 3 per cent studied upto Inter and significantly, 30 percent have high academic qualifications.

In Ambajipeta mandal out of 78 respondents, 26 per cent are restored and significantly majority (74 per cent) are not-restored (Refer Table-5.3(a). Among the restored, 35 per cent are illiterates, 5 per cent studied upto primary 10 per cent studied upto Upper Primary, 30 per cent studied upto Secondary and 20 per cent have high academic qualifications.

Whereas, among the not-restored, 47 per cent are illiterates, 22 per cent studied upto Primary, 5 per cent studied upto Upper Primary, 10 per cent studied upto

Table 5.3: Literacy Levels-Restoration.

A: Illiterate B: Primary C: Upper Primary D: Secondary E: Inter F: Degree G: Other TR: Total Respondents

Mandal	*Restored*							
	A	*B*	*C*	*D*	*E*	*F*	*G*	*Total restored*
Amalapuram	6 (13.3) (3.2)	14 (31.2) (12.7)	6 (13.3) (13.4)	6 (13.3) (14.7)	2 (4.4) (15.4)	7 (15.6) (29.2)	4 (8.9) (57.1)	45 (100.0) (10.5)
Amabajipeta	7 (35.0) (3.7)	1 (5.0) (0.9)	2 (10.0) (4.4)	6 (30.0) (14.7)	0 (0.0) (0.0)	4 (20.0) (16.6)	0 (0.0) (0.0)	20 (100.0) (4.7)
I. Polavaram	70 (55.6) (37.0)	20 (15.9) (18.2)	16 (12.7) (35.6)	9 (7.1) (21.9)	4 (3.2) (30.7)	7 (5.5) (29.5)	0 (0.0) (0.0)	126 (100.0) (29.4)
Ainavilli	40 (26.5) (21.2)	58 (38.4) (52.7)	20 (13.2) (44.4)	19 (12.6) (46.3)	5 (3.3) (38.5)	6 (4.0) (25.0)	3 (2.0) (42.9)	151 (100.0) (35.2)
Katrenikona	66 (76.0) (34.9)	17 (19.5) (15.5)	1 (1.1) (2.2)	1 (1.1) (2.4)	2 (2.3) (15.4)	0 (0.0) (0.0)	0 (0.0) (0.0)	87 (100.0) (20.2)
Total	**189 (44.1) (100.0)**	**110 (25.6) (100.0)**	**45 (10.5) (100.0)**	**41 (9.6) (100.0)**	**13 (3.0) (100.0)**	**24 (5.6) (100.0)**	**7 (1.6) (100.0)**	**429 (100.0) (100.0)**

(Table Contd...)

Table 5.3: Contd...

Mandal	*Not restored*							*Total not-restored*	*Grand Total*
	A	*B*	*C*	*D*	*E*	*F*	*G*		
Amalapuram	6 (15.0) (6.3)	11 (27.5) (32.4)	3 (7.5) (50.0)	7 (17.5) (50.0)	1 (2.5) (33.3)	9 (22.5) (60.0)	3 (7.5) (75.0)	40 (100.0) (23.4)	85
Amabajipeta	27 (46.6) (28.4)	13 (22.4) (38.2)	3 (5.2) (50.0)	6 (10.3) (42.9)	2 (3.4) (66.7)	6 (10.3) (40.0)	1 (1.7) (25.0)	58 (100.0) (33.9)	78
I. Polavaram	4 (80.0) (4.3)	0 (0.0) (0.0)	0 (0.0) (0.0)	1 (20.0) (7.1)	0 (0.0) (0.0)	0 (0.0) (0.0)	0 (0.0) (0.0)	5 (100.0) (2.9)	131
Ainavilli	8 (66.7) (8.4)	4 (33.3) (11.8)	0 (0.0) (0.0)	0 (0.0) (0.0)	0 (0.0) (0.0)	0 (0.0) (0.0)	0 (0.0) (0.0)	12 (100.0) (7.0)	163
Katrenikona	50 (89.3) (52.6)	6 (10.7) (17.6)	0 (0.0) (0.0)	0 (0.0) (0.0)	0 (0.0) (0.0)	0 (0.0) (0.0)	0 (0.0) (0.0)	56 (100.0) (32.8)	143
Total	**95 (55.6)** **(100.0)**	**34 (19.9)** **(100.0)**	**6 (3.5)** **(100.0)**	**14 (8.2)** **(100.0)**	**3 (1.8)** **(100.0)**	**15 (8.8)** **(100.0)**	**4 (2.2)** **(100.0)**	**171(100.0)** **(100.0)**	**600**

(figures in horizontal parentheses indicate percentages with regard to restored and not-restored)
(figures in vertical parentheses indicate percentages with regard to literacy)

Secondary, 3 per cent studied upto Inter, and 12 per cent have high academic qualifications.

Table 5.3 (a): Mandal-wise Restoration.

Mandal	*Restored*	*Not-restored*	*Total*
Amalapuram	45 (52.9)	40 (47.1)	85 (100.0)
Ambajipeta	20 (25.6)	58 (74.4)	78 (100.0)
I. Polavaram	126 (96.2)	5 (3.8)	131 (100.0)
Ainavilli	151 (92.6)	12 (7.4)	163 (100.0)
Katrenikona	87 (60.8)	56 (39.2)	143 (100.0)
Total	**429 (71.5)**	**171 (28.5)**	**600 (100.0)**

Table 5.3 (b): Literacy Levels-Restoration.

Literacy Levels	*Restored*	*Not- restored*	*Total*
Illiterate	189 (31.5)	95 (15.8)	284 (47.3)
Primary	110 (18.3)	34 (5.7)	144 (24.0)
Upper Primary	45 (7.5)	6 (1.0)	51 (8.5)
Secondary	41 (6.8)	14 (2.3)	55 (9.2)
Inter	13 (2.2)	3 (0.5)	16 (2.7)
Degree	24 (4.0)	15 (2.5)	39 (6.5)
Others	7 (1.2)	4 (0.6)	11 (1.8)
Total	**429 (71.5)**	**171 (28.5)**	**600 (100.0)**

In I. Polavaram mandal, out of 131 respondents, majority (96 per cent) are restored and only 4 per cent are not-restored. Among the restored, 56 per cent are illiterates, 16 per cent studied upto Primary, 13 per cent studied upto Upper Primary, 7 per cent studied upto secondary, 3 per cent studied upto Inter and only 5 per cent have high academic qualifications. Whereas among the not-restored, 80 per cent are illiterates and the other 20 per cent studied upto Secondary Education.

In Ainavilli mandal out of 163 respondents, majority (93 per cent) are restored and only 7 per cent are not-restored. Among the restored respondents, 27 per cent are illiterate, 38 per cent studied upto Primary, 13 per cent each studied upto Upper Primary and Secondary, 3 per cent studied upto Inter and 6 per cent have high academic qualifications.

Whereas, among the not-restored respondents, majority (67 per cent) are illiterates and the remaining (33 per cent) studied upto Primary.

In Katrenikona mandal, out of 143 respondents, majority (61 per cent) are restored and 39 per cent are not-restored. Among the restored respondents, majority (76 per cent) are illiterates, 20 per cent studied upto Primary, one per cent each studied upto Upper Primary, and Secondary and another two per cent studied upto Inter.

Whereas among the not-restored respondents, majority (89 per cent) are illiterates and the remaining 11 per cent studied upto Primary.

The overall scenario of restored respondents (71.5 per cent) shows that among them, 44 per cent are illiterates, 26 percent studied upto Primary, 11 per cent studied upto Upper Primary, 10 per cent studied upto Secondary, 3 per cent studied upto Inter and only 7 per cent have high academic qualifications.

Whereas the overall not-restored scenario show that, among them, majority (56 per cent) are illiterates (28.5 per cent) 20 per cent studied upto Primary, 3 per cent studied upto Upper Primary, 8 per cent studied upto Secondary, 2 per cent studied upto Inter and, significantly, 11 per cent have high academic qualifications.

The following observations can be made with regard to literacy levels and restoration of the respondents:

1. There are differences from mandal to mandal with regard to restoration, even though majority of the respondents are restored (71.5 per cent). As presented in Table-5.4 (a) I. Polavaram mandal

has the highest percentage (96 per cent) of restored respondents followed by Ainavilli mandal (93 per cent), Katrenikona mandal (61 per cent) and Amalapuram mandal (53 per cent). The restoration position in Ambajipeta mandal is worse with 74 per cent not-restored respondents.

2. As there are differences from mandal to mandal, there are also differences with regard to literacy levels and restoration:

   (a) Among the restored respondents (71.5 per cent) literates are 56 per cent and illiterates are 44 per cent. Among the restored, 7 per cent have high academic qualifications. Out of the total illiterate restored respondents more number are in Katrenikona mandal (35 per cent). Out of the total highly literate restored respondents more majority are in Amalapuram mandal (43 per cent).

   (b) Among the not-restored respondents (28.5 per cent) illiterates are in majority (56 per cent) and literates are 44 per cent. Among the not-restored, 11 per cent have high academic qualifications. Out of the total illiterate not-restored respondents, majority (53 per cent) are in Katrenikona mandal. Out of the total highly literate not-restored respondents, majority (68 per cent) are in Amalapuram mandal.

   (c) In comparison, we can say that more number of literates are restored than the illiterates and interestingly highly qualified group are more in not-restored group.

3.

   (a) Out of the total 600 respondents (Refer [Table-5.3(b)], restored respondents (68 per cent) are

illiterates; the restored respondents with high academic qualifications are 5 per cent.

(b) More number of not-restored are illiterates (16 per cent) followed by 6 per cent of Primary level respondents. The not-restored respondents with high academic qualifications are only 3 per cent.

(c) On the whole, literates (53 per cent) topped the total sample of 600. The primary level (44 per cent) respondents are more among the literates.

(d) In comparison, the literates that too more with high academic qualifications are restored more.

4. There is close association between literacy levels and restoration.

Occupation Structure-Restoration

Out of the total sample of 600 respondents, 429 (71.5 per cent) are restored and 171 (28.5 per cent) are not-restored. In Table-5.4, occupation structure in relation to restoration of the respondents is presented (for Table see at the end of the chapter).

In Amalapuram mandal, out of 85 respondents, 53 per cent are restored and 47 per cent are not-restored. Among the restored respondents, 16 per cent (9 per cent +7 per cent) have agriculture and coconut plantations, 4 per cent settled in private jobs, 13 per cent are doing Government jobs, a little less than half (49 per cent) are weavers, 7 per cent each are self-employed and service job-holders and only 4 percent are agricultural labourers.

Whereas among the not-restored, 28 per cent are in agriculture and coconut plantation (8 per cent + 20 per cent) another 28 percent are in Government service, 18 per

Table 5.4: Occupation Structure-Restoration.

A: Agriculture B: Coconut Plantation C: Private Job D: Government Service E: Weaving F: Self Employment G: Fishing H: Service I: Agricultural Labour

Mandal	*Restored*									*Total*
	A	B	C	D	E	F	G	H	I	*restored*
Amalapuram	4 (8.9) (2.9)	3 (6.7) (7.1)	2 (4.4) (40.0)	6 (13.3) (40.0)	22 (48.9) (100.0)	3 (6.7) (15.8)	0 (0.0) (0.0)	3 (6.7) (23.0)	2 (4.4) (1.7)	45 (100.0) (10.5)
Ambajipeta	2 (10.0) (1.4)	5 (25.0) (11.9)	1 (5.0) (20.0)	2 (10.0) (13.3)	0 (0.0) (0.0)	0 (0.0) (0.0)	0 (0.0) (0.0)	1 (5.0) (7.7)	9 (45.0) (7.8)	20 (100.0) (4.7)
I. Polavaram	45 (35.7) (32.6)	10 (7.9) (23.8)	1 (0.8) (20.0)	3 (2.4) (20.0)	0 (0.0) (0.0)	8 (6.3) (42.1)	37 (29.4) (61.7)	2 (1.6) (15.4)	20 (15.9) (17.4)	126 (100.0) (29.4)
Ainavilli	47 (31.1) (34.1)	22 (14.6) (52.4)	1 (0.7) (20.0)	3 (2.0) (20.0)	0 (0.0) (0.0)	6 (4.0) (31.6)	3 (2.0) (5.0)	5 (3.3) (38.5)	64 (42.3) (55.7)	151 (100.0) (35.2)
Katrenikona	40 (46.0) (29.0)	2 (2.3) (4.8)	0 (0.0) (0.0)	1 (1.1) (6.7)	0 (0.0) (0.0)	2 (2.3) (10.5)	20 (23.0) (33.3)	2 (2.3) (15.4)	20 (23.0) (17.4)	87 (100.0) (20.2)
Total	**138(32.2) (100.0)**	**42 (9.8) (100.0)**	**5 (1.2) (100.0)**	**15 (3.5) (100.0)**	**22 (5.1) (100.0)**	**19 (4.4) (100.0)**	**60 (14.0) (100.0)**	**13 (3.0) (100.0)**	**115 (26.8) (100.0)**	**429 (100.0) (100.0)**

(Table Contd...)

Table 5.4: Contd...

Mandal	*Not-Restored*									*Total*
	A	*B*	*C*	*D*	*E*	*F*	*G*	*H*	*I*	*restored*
Amalapuram	3 (7.5) (10.3)	8 (20.0) (34.8)	1 (2.5) (50.0)	11 (27.5) (55.0)	2 (5.0) (50.0)	1 (2.5) (100.0)	0 (0.0) (0.0)	7 (17.5) (58.3)	7 (17.5) (14.3)	40 (100.0) (23.4)
Ambajipeta	3 (5.2) (10.3)	12 (20.7) (52.2)	1 (1.7) (50.0)	8 (18.9) (40.0)	1 (1.7) (25.0)	0 (0.0) (0.0)	0 (0.0) (0.0)	4 (6.8) (33.3)	29 (50.0) (59.2)	58 (100.0) (33.9)
I. Polavaram	0 (0.0) (0.0)	0 (0.0) (0.0)	0 (0.0) (0.0)	1 (20.0) (5.0)	0 (0.0) (0.0)	0 (0.0) (0.0)	3 (60.0) (9.7)	0 (0.0) (0.0)	1 (20.0) (2.0)	5 (100.0) (2.9)
Ainavilli	7 (58.3) (24.1)	1 (8.3) (4.3)	0 (0.0) (0.0)	0 (0.0) (0.0)	1 (8.3) (25.0)	0 (0.0) (0.0)	0 (0.0) (0.0)	0 (0.0) (0.0)	3 (25.0) (6.1)	12 (100.0) (7.0)
Katrenikona	16 (28.2) (55.2)	2 (3.6) (8.7)	0 (0.0) (0.0)	0 (0.0) (0.0)	0 (0.0) (0.0)	0 (0.0) (0.0)	28 (50.0) (90.3)	1 (1.8) (8.4)	9 (16.0) (18.4)	56 (100.0) (32.8)
Total	**29 (16.9)** **(100.0)**	**23 (13.5)** **(100.0)**	**2 (1.2)** **(100.0)**	**20 (11.7)** **(100.0)**	**4 (2.3)** **(100.0)**	**1 (0.6)** **(100.0)**	**31 (18.1)** **(100.0)**	**12 (7.0)** **(100.0)**	**49 (28.7)** **(100.0)**	**171 (100.0)** **(100.0)**

(figures in horizontal parentheses indicate percentages with regard to restored and not-restored)
(figures in vertical parentheses indicate percentages with regard to occupation)

cent each are in service occupations and as agricultural labourers and insignificant percentage of agricultural labourers and insignificant percentage of respondents are in private jobs, self-employment and weaving.

In Ambajipeta mandal, out of 78 respondents, a little above one-fourth (26 per cent) are restored and majority (74 per cent) are not-restored. Among the restored, 35 per cent are doing agriculture (10 per cent + 25 per cent) 5 per cent each are doing private jobs and service occupations, 10 per cent are doing Government jobs and significantly 45 per cent are working as agricultural labourers.

Whereas among the not-restored respondents, 26 per cent are in agriculture and coconut plantation (5 per cent + 21 per cent), 19 per cent are in Government jobs, majority (50 per cent) are working as agricultural labourers, 7 per cent are doing service occupations and 3 per cent are doing private jobs and weaving.

In I. Polavaram mandal, out of 131 respondents majority (96 per cent) are restored and only 4 per cent are not-restored. Among the restored, 44 per cent are in the field of agriculture and coconut plantation (36 per cent + 8 per cent), 29 per cent are in fishing, 16 per cent are as agricultural labours and the remaining are in private jobs, Government jobs, self-employment and service occupations.

Whereas among the not-restored respondents, majority are in fishing followed by private jobs and agricultural labourers.

In Ainavilli mandal, out of 163 respondents, majority (93 per cent) are restored and only 7' per cent are not-restored. Among the restored, 46 per cent (31 per cent + 15 per cent) are in the field of agriculture and coconut plantation, 42 per cent are agricultural labourers and the remaining (12 per cent) are in private jobs, Government jobs, self-employment, fishing and service occupations.

Whereas among the not-restored respondents, majority (67 per cent) are in the field of agriculture, 25 per cent are agricultural labourers and the remaining 8 per cent are in weaving.

In Katrenikona mandal, out of 143 respondents, 61 per cent are restored and 39 per cent are not-restored. Among the restored respondents, 48 per cent are in the field of agriculture, 23 per cent are in fishing and another 23 per cent are agricultural labourers and the remaining 6 per cent are in private jobs, self-employment and service occupations.

Whereas among the not-restored respondents, majority (50 per cent) are in fishing, 33 per cent are in the fields of agriculture and coconut plantation (29 per cent + 4 per cent), 16 per cent are agricultural labourers and the remaining 2 per cent are in service occupations.

The overall scenario of 429 restored respondents (71.5 per cent) shows that 42 per cent (32 per cent + 10 per cent) are in the field of agriculture and coconut plantation, 27 per cent are agricultural labourers, 14 per cent are in fishing and the remaining 17 per cent are doing other kinds of jobs.

Whereas the overall scenario of 171 not-restored respondents (28.5 per cent) shows that among them more number are (31 per cent) in the field of agriculture, followed by agricultural labourers (29 per cent) fishing (18 per cent), and 11 per cent in Government jobs. And the remaining 11 per cent are in private jobs and weaving.

The following observations can be made basing on occupation and restoration of the respondents:

1. There are differences from mandal to mandal with regard to restoration even though majority (71.5 per cent) are restored in the total sample. As explained in Table-5.4(a), I. Polavaram mandal

has the highest percentage (96 per cent) of restored respondents followed by Ainavilli mandal (93 per cent), Katrenikona mandal (61 per cent), and Amalapuram mandal (53 per cent). The restoration position in Ambajipeta mandal is worse than in other mandals. Ambajipeta mandal topped with 74 per cent not-restored respondents followed by Amalapuram mandal (47 per cent) and Katrenikona mandal (39 per cent).

Table 5.4 (a): Mandal-wise Restoration.

Mandal	*Restored*	*Not-restored*	*Total*
Amalapuram	45 (52.9)	40 (47.1)	85 (100.0)
Ambajipeta	20 (25.6)	58 (74.4)	78 (100.0)
I. Polavaram	126 (96.2)	5 (3.8)	131 (100.0)
Ainavilli	151 (92.6)	12 (7.4)	163 (100.0)
Katrenikona	87 (60.8)	56 (39.2)	143 (100.0)
Total	**429 (71.5)**	**171 (28.5)**	**600 (100.0)**

2. As there are differences from mandal to mandal with regard to restoration, there are also differences with regard to occupation structure of the respondents:

   (a) Majority (71.5 per cent) of the total 600 respondents are restored while only 28.5 per cent are not-restored. Among the total restored, agriculture has been the main occupation for the majority (42 per cent) followed by Agricultural labour (27 pr cent) and fishing (14 per cent). The respondents with agriculture as their occupation are restored more in Ainavilli mandal (43 per cent) and the respondents working as agricultural labourers who are restored are also more in Ainavilli mandal (56 per cent). The respondents with fishing as their major

occupation are restored more in I. Polavaram mandal with 62 per cent.

(b) Among the not-restored (28.5 per cent) also agriculture topped the list (31 per cent), followed by agricultural labour (29 per cent) and fishing (18 per cent). In not-restored category also the respondents with agriculture as their occupation topped the list and in Ambajipeta mandal (31 per cent) more number in agriculture as well as in agricultural labour (59 per cent) are not restored. The respondents with fishing as their occupation who are not restored are in majority in Katrenikona mandal (90 per cent).

(c) Interesingly in comparison the Government job-holders who happened to be secure in their positions are more (12 per cent) among not-restored group than in restored group (4 per cent).

3.

(a) Out of the 600 total size of the sample (Refer Table-5.4 (b)] more number (30 per cent) are in the field of agriculture followed by agricultural labour (19 per cent) and fishing (10 per cent).

(b) More number of not-restored (9 per cent) are also in the field of agriculture followed by agricultural labour (8 per cent) and fishing (5 per cent).

(c) Except the respondents in Government service and in all other fields restored are more than not-restored.

Table 5.4 (b): Occupation Structure-Restoration.

Occupation	*Restored*	*Not- restored*	*Total*
Agriculture	138 (23.0)	29 (4.8)	167 (27.8)
Coconut Plantation	42 (7.0)	23 (3.8)	65 (10.8)
Private jobs	5 (0.8)	2 (0.3)	7 (1.2)
Govt. Service	15 (2.5)	20 (3.3)	35 (5.8)
Weaving	22 (3.7)	4 (0.6)	26 (4.3)
Self-employment	19 (3.2)	1 (0.1)	20 (3.3)
Fishing	60 (10.0)	31 (5.3)	91 (15.3)
Service occupations	13 (2.2)	12 (2.0)	25 (4.2)
Agricultural labour	115 (19.2)	49 (8.1)	164 (27.3)
Total	**429 (71.5)**	**171 (28.5)**	**600 (100.0)**

(d) Relatively more number of Government servants are not-restored.

(e) And half of the respondents as fishing as their major occupation are not-restored.

4. It is quite natural that agricultural labourers and fishermen who belonged to low income groups are not-restored.

Total Household Income-Restoration

Out of the 600 total sample, 71.5 per cent are restored and 28.5 per cent are not-restored. In Table-5.5, total household income of the respondents in relation to restoration is presented in Table-5.5, Table-5.5(a) and Table-5.5(b) (See at the end of the chapter).

In Amalapuram mandal, out of 85 respondents, 53 per cent are restored and compared to 47 per cent of not-restored respondents. Among the restored, 11 per cent belonged to highest income group (i.e., F+G = Rs.45,000-65,000), majority (60 per cent) belonged to middle income group (i.e., C+D+E = Rs.15,000-45,000) and 29 per cent belonged to low income category.

Table 5.5: Total Household Income-Restoration.

A: <5000 B: 5000-15,000 C: 15,000-25,000 D: 25,000-35,000 E: 35,000-45000 F: 45,000-55,000 G: 55,000-65,000
TR: Total Respondent

Mandal	*Restored*							
	A	*B*	*C*	*D*	*E*	*F*	*G*	*T*
Amalapuram	1 (2.2)	12(26.7)	19(42.2)	4 (8.9)	4 (8.9)	0 (0.0)	5(11.1)	45(100.0)
	(2.3)	(5.2)	(23.8)	(11.4)	(21.1)	(0.0)	(33.3)	(10.5)
Ambajipeta	0 (0.0)	13(65.0)	3 (15.0)	1 (5.0)	0 (0.0)	0 (0.0)	3(15.0)	20(100.0)
	(0.0)	(5.7)	(3.8)	(2.9)	(0.0)	(0.0)	(20.0)	(4.7)
I. Polavaram	13(10.3)	47(37.3)	28(22.2)	19(15.1)	10(7.9)	4 (3.2)	5 (4.0)	126(100.0)
	(30.2)	(20.5)	(35.0)	(54.3)	(52.6)	(50.0)	(33.3)	(29.4)
Ainavilli	4 (2.6)	102(67.5)	26(17.3)	9 (6.1)	4 (2.6)	4 (2.6)	2 (13.4)	151(100.0)
	(9.3)	(44.6)	(32.4)	(25.7)	(21.1)	(50.0)		(35.2)
Katrenikona	25(28.7)	55 (63.3)	4 (4.6)	2 (2.3)	1 (1.1)	0 (0.0)	0 (0.0)	87(100.0)
	(58.2)	(24.0)	(5.0)	(5.7)	(5.2)	(0.0)	(0.0)	(20.2)
Total	**43(10.0)**	**229(53.4)**	**80(18.6)**	**35 (8.2)**	**19(4.4)**	**8 (1.9)**	**15(3.56)**	**429(100.0)**
	(100.0)	**(100.0)**	**(100.0)**	**(100.0)**	**(100.0)**	**(100.0)**	**(100.0)**	**(100.0)**

(Table Contd...)

Table 5.5: Contd...

Mandal	*Not Restored*							
	A	*B*	*C*	*D*	*E*	*F*	*G*	*TR*
Amalapuram	0 (0.0)	20(250.0)	6(15.0)	3(7.5)	0(0.0)	1(2.5)	10(25.0)	40(100.0)
	(0.0)	(18.2)	(33.3)	(50.0)	(0.0)	(50.0)	(43.5)	(2304)
Ambajipeta	0 (0.0)	37(63.8)	6(10.3)	2(3.4)	0 (0.0)	0(0.0)	13(22.4)	58(100.0)
	(0.0)	(33.6)	(33.3)	(33.3)	(0.0)	(0.0)	(56.5)	(33.9)
I. Polavaram	1 (20.0)	3(60.0)	0(0.0)	0(0.0)	0 (0.0)	1(20.0)	0 (0.0)	5(100.0)
	(8.3)	(2.7)	(0.0)	(0.0)	(0.0)	(50.0)	(0.0)	(2.9)
Ainavilli	1 (8.3)	10(83.4)	1(8.3)	0 (0.0)	0 (0.0)	0 (0.0)	0 (0.0)	12(100.0)
	(8.3)	(9.1)	(5.6)	(0.0)	(0.0)	(0.0)	(0.0)	(7.0)
Katrenikona	10(17.9)	40(71.4)	5(8.9)	1(1.8)	0 (0.0)	0 (0.0)	0 (0.0)	56(100.0)
	(83.4)	(36.4)	(27.8)	(16.7)	(0.0)	(0,0)	(0.0)	(32.8)
Total	**12(7.0)**	**110(64.3)**	**18(10.5)**	**6(3.5)**	**0 (0.0)**	**2(1.2)**	**23(13.5)**	**171(100.0)**
	(100.0)	**(100.0)**	**(100.0)**	**(3.5)**	**(0.0)**	**(100.0)**	**(100.0)**	**(100.0)**

(figures in horizontal parentheses indicate percentages with regard to restored and not-restored)
(figures in vertical parentheses indicate percentages with regard to income)

Table 5.5 (a): Mandal-wise Restoration.

Mandal	*Restored*	*Not-restored*	*Total*
Amalapuram	45 (52.9)	40 (47.1)	85 (100.0)
Ambajipeta	20 (25.6)	58 (74.4)	78 (100.0)
I. Polavaram	126 (96.2)	5 (3.8)	131 (100.0)
Ainavilli	151 (92.6)	12 (7.4)	163 (100.0)
Katrenikona	87 (60.8)	56 (39.2)	143 (100.0)
Total	**429 (71.5)**	**171 (28.5)**	**600 (100.0)**

Table 5.5 (b): Total Household Income-Restoration.

Occupation	*Restored*	*Not- restored*	*Total*
< 5000	43 (7.2)	12 (2.0)	55 (9.2)
5000-15000	229 (38.2)	110 (18.3)	339 (56.5)
15000-25000	80 (13.3)	18 (3.0)	98 (16.3)
25000-35000	35 (5.8)	6 (1.0)	41 (6.8)
35000-45000	19 (3.2)	0 (0.0)	19 (3.2)
45000-55-000	8 (1.3)	2 (0.3)	10 (1.7)
55000-65000	15 (2.5)	23 (3.8)	38 (6.3)
Total	**429 (71.5)**	**171 (28.5)**	**600 (100.0)**

Whereas among the not-restored, 28 per cent belonged to the highest income group, 22 per cent belonged to middle income group and majority belonged to low income group.

In Ambajipeta mandal out of 78 respondents only 26 per cent are restored and 74 per cent are not restored. Among the restored, 15 per cent belonged to the highest income group, 20 per cent belonged to the middle income group and majority (65 per cent) belonged to the low income group.

Whereas among the not-restored respondents, 22 per cent belonged to the highest income group, 14 per cent belonged to the middle income group and majority (64 per cent) belonged to the low income group.

In I. Polavaram mandal, out of 131 respondents, 96 per cent are restored and only 4 per cent are not restored. Among the restored respondents, 45 per cent belonged to the middle income group and 48 per cent belonged to the low income group.

Whereas among the not restored respondents, 20 per cent belonged to the highest income group and majority (80 per cent) belonged to the low income group.

In Ainavilli mandal, out of 163 respondents only 4 per cent belonged to the highest income group, 26 per cent belonged to the middle income group and majority (70 per cent) belonged to the low income group.

Whereas among the not restored respondents, only 8 per cent belonged to the middle income group and majority (92 per cent) belonged to the low income group.

In Katrenikona mandal, out of 143 respondents, only 7 per cent belonged to the middle income group and all the rest (93 per cent) belonged to low income group.

Whereas among the not restored respondents, only 11 per cent belonged to middle income group and all the rest 89 per cent belonged to low income group.

The overall scenario of the restored respondents (71.5 per cent) shows that only 6 percent belonged to highest income group, 31 per cent belonged to middle income group and majority (63 per cent) belonged to low income group.

Whereas the overall scenario of not restored respondent (28.5 per cent) shows that 15 per cent belonged to highest income group, 14 per cent belonged to middle income group and majority (71 per cent) belonged to low income group.

The following observations can be made based on the total household income of the respondents, along with restoration:

1. There are differences from mandal to mandal with regard to restoration, even though majority (71.5 per cent) are restored in the total sample. As explained in Table-5.5(a), I. Polavaram mandal has the highest restored respondents (96 per cent), followed by Ainavilli mandal (93 per cent), Katrenikona mandal (61 per cent), Amalapuram mandal (53 per cent). And majority of the respondents in Ambajipeta mandal (74 per cent) are not restored followed by Amalapuram mandal (47 per cent) and Katrenikona mandal (39 per cent).

2. As we noticed mandal-wise differences, we also noticed income-wise differences in terms of restoration.

   (a) Out of 429 (71.5 per cent) restored respondents, majority belonged to total household income group of Rs.5000-15000. More number of respondents in I. Polavaram mandal (42 per cent) belonged to the highest income groups (i.e., 45,000-65,000). More number (47 per cent) respondents in Katrenikona mandal (41 per cent) belonged to low income group (Rs.<5000-15,000) (Refer vertical percentages in Table-5.5).

   (b) Out of 171 (28.5 per cent) not restored respondents, majority (64 per cent) belonged to Rs.5,000-15,000 income group. More number (47 per cent) of respondents in Amalapuram mandal belonged to the highest income group as well as middle income groups (42 per cent). And majority of not restored respondents in Katrenikona mandal (60 per cent) belonged to the low income groups.

(c) Even though there is differences of comparison with regard to restored and not restored respondents and their total income levels, one interesting point is that more numbers in Ambajipeta and Amalapuram mandals who belonged to highest income groups are not restored. The more the assets in the from of lands, the high is the loss and takes time for further restoration may be true in this case.

3. Out of 600 total size of the sample, majority are restored (71.5 per cent),

   (a) Out of 600, 38 per cent who are restored belonged to Rs.5000-15000 income group and 18 per cent of not restored also belonged to Rs.5000-15000 income group.

   (b) Compared to restored and not restored respondents, the restored respondents are more in low and middle income groups, but interestingly the comparative figure is more in not restored respondents in high income groups (3.8 per cent to 4.1 per cent).

4. But, there is no much relation between total household income and restoration.

Part-B

Caste-wise Opinions on Rehabilitation

In Table-5.6, Rehabilitation of respondents in relation to caste is presented (for table see at the end of the chapter). Based on the presentation, the following observations can be made:

1. Out of the total sample of 600 respondents, only 3 per cent felt very happy, 5 per cent felt happy,

Table 5.6: Caste-wise opinions on Rehabilitation.

Mandal	Very Happy					Happy				
	F.C.	B.C.	S.C.	S.T.	TR	F.C.	B.C.	S.C.	S.T.	TR
Amalapuram	3	4	1	0	8 (1.3)	10	16	1	0	27 (4.5)
Ambajipeta	4	0	0	0	4 (0.7)	9	3	16	1	29 (4.8)
I. Polavaram	1	0	0	0	1 (0.2)	37	42	11	1	91 (15.2)
Ainavilli	3	1	1	0	5 (0.8)	26	11	38	0	75 (12.5)
Katrenikona	0	0	1	0	1 (0.2)	14	64	44	0	122 (20.3)
Total	**11 (1.8)**	**5 (0.8)**	**3 (0.5)**	**0 (0.0)**	**19 (3.2)**	**96 (16.0)**	**136 (22.7)**	**110 (18.3)**	**2 (0.3)**	**344 (57.3)**

(Table Contd...)

Table 5.6: Contd...

Mandal	Satisfactory					Unhappy					Very Unhappy					Total
	F.C.	B.C.	S.C.	S.T.	TR	F.C.	B.C.	S.C.	S.T.	TR	F.C.	B.C.	S.C.	S.T.	TR	
Amalapuram	4	7	1	0	12 (2.0)	13	15	0	0	28 (4.7)	4	4	2	0	10 (1.6)	85
Ambajipeta	2	0	2	0	4 (0.6)	9	4	5	4	22 (3.7)	9	5	3	2	19 (3.2)	78
I. Polavaram	3	5	2	0	10 (1.7)	17	6	3	0	26 (4.3)	2	1	0	0	3 (0.5)	131
Ainavilli	1	3	4	0	8 (1.3)	24	23	19	0	66 (11.0)	2	4	3	0	9 (1.5)	163
Katrenikona	4	4	2	0	10 (1.7)	0	3	1	0	4 (0.7)	2	1	3	0	6 (1.0)	143
Total	**14 (2.3)**	**19 (3.2)**	**11 (1.8)**	**0 (0.0)**	**44 (7.3)**	**63 (10.5)**	**51 (8.5)**	**28 (4.7)**	**4 (0.7)**	**146 (24.4)**	**19 (3.2)**	**15 (2.5)**	**11 (1.8)**	**2 (0.3)**	**47 (7.8)**	**600**

7 per cent felt satisfactory, 24 per cent felt unhappy and 8 per cent felt very unhappy regarding the rehabilitation facilities.

2. Among the respondents who felt very happy are more among Forward Castes (1.8 per cent). The respondents who felt happy are more among Backward Castes (23 per cent). The respondents who felt satisfactory are also more among Backward Castes (3 per cent). The respondents who felt unhappy are more among Forward Castes (11 per cent). And the respondents waho felt very unhappy are also more among Forward Castes (3.0 per cent).

3. The mandal-wise scenario shows that respondents who felt very happy are more in Amalapuram mandal (1.3 per cent). The respondents who felt happy are more in Katrenikone mandal (20 per cent). The respondents who felt satisfactory are also more in Amalapuram mandal (2 per cent). The respondents who felt unhappy are more in Ainavilli mandal (11 per cent). And the respondents who felt very unhappy are more in Ambajipeta mandal (3 per cent).

4.

(*a*) The opinions of Forward Castes with regard to rehabilitation prograammes shows that more number of Forward Castes respondents (16 per cent) felt happy.

(*b*) The opinions of Backward Castes respondents with regard to rehabilitation programmes shows that more number (23 per cent) of Backward Caste respondents too felt happy.

(*c*) The opinions of Scheduled Castes respondents

shows that more number among them too (18 per cent) felt happy with regard to rehabilitation programmes.

(d) The opinions of Scheduled Tribes shows that more number (0.7 per cent) felt unhappy with regard to rehabilitation programmes.

5. Majority of the respondents (57 per cent) felt happy with regard to rehabilitation programmes except the Scheduled Tribe respondents. At the same time, one-fourth of the total respondents felt unhappy and 8 per cent felt very unhappy with the programmes, which needs further attention of the government in the management of natural disasters like cyclones.

Age-opinions on Rehabilitation Programmes

In Table-5.7, Rehabilitation of respondents in relation to age is presented (See at the end of the chapter). Based on the presentation the following observations may be made:

1. Out of the total sample of 600 respondents only 3 per cent felt very happy, majority (5.7 per cent) felt happy, 7 per cent felt satisfactory, 24 per cent felt unhappy and 8 per cent felt very unhappy regarding the rehabilitation facilities.

2. The respondents who felt very happy are more among 40-41 age group (1.5 per cent). The respondents who felt happy are also more among 40-49 age-group 17.2 per cent). The respondents who felt satisfactory are more among 50-59 age group (2.2 per cent). The respondents who felt unhappy are also more among 40-49 age group (7.5 per cent). The respondents who felt very unhappy are also more among 40-49 age group (2.3 per cent).

Table 5.7: Age-Groups (Opinions on Rehabilitation Facilities).

A: (20-29) B: (30-39) C: (40-49) D: (50-59) E: (60-69) F: (70-79)

Mandal	*Very Happy*							*Happy*							*Satisfactory*			
	A	*B*	*C*	*D*	*E*	*F*	*TR*	*A*	*B*	*C*	*D*	*E*	*F*	*TR*	*A*	*B*	*C*	*D*
Amalapuram	0	2	4	0	2	2	8 (1.3)	2	8	9	7	1	0	27 (4.5)	0	2	2	5
Ambajipeta	0	0	2	0	0	0	4 (0.7)	4	7	7	8	5	1	29 (4.8)	0	1	0	1
I. Polavaram	0	0	1	0	0	0	1 (0.2)	4	41	25	12	8	1	91 (15.2)	0	4	3	1
Ainavilli	0	1	2	1	0	0	5 (0.8)	3	13	27	13	16	3	75 (12.5)	1	3	2	2
Katrenikona	0	0	0	0	1	1	1 (0.2)	16	26	38	17	20	5	122 (20.3)	1	2	2	4
Total	**0** **(0.0)**	**3** **(0.5)**	**9** **(1.5)**	**1** **(0.2)**	**3** **(0.5)**	**3** **(0.5)**	**19** **(3.2)**	**29** **(4.8)**	**95** **(15.8)**	**103** **(17.2)**	**57** **(9.5)**	**50** **(8.3)**	**10** **(1.7)**	**344** **(57.3)**	**2** **(0.3)**	**12** **(2.0)**	**9** **(1.5)**	**13** **(2.2)**

(Table Contd...)

Table 5.7: Contd...

Mandal	Satisfactory			Un happy							Very Unhappy							Grand
	E	*F*	*TR*	*A*	*B*	*C*	*D*	*E*	*F*	*TR*	*A*	*B*	*C*	*D*	*E*	*F*	*TR*	*Total*
Amalapuram	3	0	12	3	6	12	4	3	0	28	0	2	3	5	0	0	10	85
							(2.0)			(4.7)							(1.7)	
Ambajipeta	2	0	4	1	5	5	3	5	3	22	1	2	5	4	5	1	19	78
							(0.7)			(3.7)							(3.2)	
I. Polavaram	2	0	10	2	7	6	9	1	1	26	0	1	2	0	0	0	3	131
							(1.7)			(4.3)							(0.5)	
Ainavilli	0	0	8	2	15	22	15	9	3	66	1	3	2	2	0	1	9	163
							(1.2)			(11.0)							(1.5)	
Katrenikona	1	0	10	1	3	0	0	0	0	4	2	1	2	0	1	0	6	143
							(1.7)			(0.7)							(1.0)	
Total	**8**	**0**	**44**	**9**	**36**	**45**	**31**	**18**	**7**	**146**	**4**	**9**	**14**	**11**	**6**	**3**	**47**	**600**
	(1.3)	**(0.0)**	**(7.3)**	**(1.5)**	**(6.0)**	**(7.5)**	**(5.2)**	**(3.0)**	**(1.2)**	**(24.4)**	**(0.7)**	**(1.5)**	**(2.3)**	**(1.8)**	**(1.0)**	**(1.5)**	**(7.8)**	**100.0)**

3. The mandal-wise scenario shows that the respondentss who felt very happy are more in Amalapuram mandal (1.3 per cent). The respondents who felt happy are more in Katrenikona mandal (20 per cent). The respondents who felt saatisfactory are also more in Amalapuram mandal (2 per cent). The respondents who felt unhappy are more in Ainavilli mandal (11 per cent). And the respondents who felt very unhappy are more in Ambajipeta mandal (3 per cent).

4.

   (a) The opinion of respondents in the age group of 20-29 with regard to rehabilitation programmes shows that more number (5%) felt happy.

   (b) The opinion of respondents in the age group of 30-39 with regard to rehabilitation programmes shows that more number (16%) felt happy.

   (c) The opinion of respondents in the age group of 40-49 with regard to rehabilitation programmes shows that more number (17%) felt satisfactory.

   (d) The opinion of respondents in the age group of 50-59 with regard to rehabilitation programmes shows that more number (10%) felt happy.

   (e) The opinion of repondents in the age group of 60-69 with regard to rehabilitation programmes shows that more number (8%) felt happy.

   (f) The opinion of respondents in the agae group of 70-79 with regard to rehabilitation

programmes shows that more number (2%) felt happy.

5. Overall, majority of the respondents (57 per cent) felt happy with regard to rehabilitation programmes. In all age groups also majority felt happy. The happiest respondents as well as unhappiest respondents are more in the age group of 40-49. Among the mandals more felt unhappy in Ambajipeta.

Literacy Levels: Opinions on Rehabilitation

In Table-5.8, rehabilitation of respondents in relation to caste is presented based on while the following observations can be made:

1. Out of the total sample of 600 respondents, only 3 per cent felt very happy, 57 per cent felt happy, 7 per cent felt satisfactory, 24 per cent felt

Table 5.8: Literacy Levels: (Opinions on Rehabilitation Facilities).

A: Illiteracy B: Primary C: Upper Primary D: Secondary E: Inter F: Degree G: Others TR: Total Respondents

Mandal	*Verty Happy*							
	A	*B*	*C*	*D*	*E*	*F*	*G*	*TR*
Amalapuram	2	1	2	0	1	1	1	8 (1.3)
Ambajipeta	1	1	0	1	0	0	1	4 (0.7)
I. Polavaram	0	0	1	0	0	0	0	1 (0.2)
Ainavilli	1	3	0	0	0	1	0	5 (0.8)
Katrenikona	1	0	0	0	0	0	0	1 (0.2)
Total	**5 (0.8)**	**5 (0.8)**	**3 (0.6)**	**1 (0.2)**	**1 (0.2)**	**2 (0.3)**	**2 (0.3)**	**19 (3.2)**

(Table Contd...)

Table 5.8: Contd...

Mandal	*Happy*							
	A	*B*	*C*	*D*	*E*	*F*	*G*	*TR*
Amalapuram	5	8	5	4	0	3	2	27 (4.5)
Ambajipeta	15	1	3	5	0	5	0	29 (4.8)
I. Polavaram	59	12	10	4	1	5	0	91 (15.2)
Ainavilli	33	28	8	2	1	1	2	75 (12.5)
Katrenikona	100	18	1	1	2	0	0	122 (0.3)
Total	**212 (35.2)**	**67 (11.2)**	**27 (4.5)**	**16 (2.7)**	**4 (2.7)**	**14 (2.3)**	**4 (0.7)**	**344 (57.3)**

Table 5.8: Contd...

Mandal	*Satisfactory*							
	A	*B*	*C*	*D*	*E*	*F*	*G*	*TR*
Amalapuram	2	2	0	2	0	3	3	12 (2.0)
Ambajipeta	1	1	0	1	0	1	0	4 (0.7)
I. Polavaram	5	2	1	2	0	0	0	10 (1.7)
Ainavilli	0	3	2	3	0	0	0	8 (1.2)
Katrenikona	7	3	0	0	0	0	0	10 (1.7)
Total	**15 (2.5)**	**11 (1.7)**	**3 (0.6)**	**8 (1.2)**	**0 (0.0)**	**4 (0.7)**	**3 (0.6)**	**44 (7.3)**

Table 5.8: Contd...

Mandal	*Unhappy*							
	A	*B*	*C*	*D*	*E*	*F*	*G*	*TR*
Amalapuram	1	10	2	5	1	8	1	28 (4.7)
Ambajipeta	9	7	1	2	2	1	0	22 (3.7)

(Table Contd...)

Table 5.8: Contd...

Mandal	*Unhappy*							
	A	*B*	*C*	*D*	*E*	*F*	*G*	*TR*
I. Polavaram	7	6	4	4	3	2	0	26 (4.3)
Ainavilli	2	24	9	14	3	3	1	66 (11.0)
Katrenikona	4	0	0	0	0	0	0	4 (0.7)
Total	**33 (5.6)**	**47 (7.8)**	**16 (2.7)**	**25 (4.2)**	**9 (1.5)**	**14 (2.3)**	**2 (0.3)**	**146 (24.4)**

Table 5.8: Contd...

Mandal	*Very Unhappy*								*Grand*
	A	*B*	*C*	*D*	*E*	*F*	*G*	*TR*	*Total*
Amalapuram	2	4	0	2	1	1	0	10 (1.7)	10 (1.7)
Ambajipeta	8	4	1	3	0	3	0	19 (3.2)	19 (3.2)
I. Polavaram	3	0	0	0	0	0	0	3 (0.5)	3 (0.5)
Ainavilli	2	4	1	0	1	1	0	9 (1.5)	9 (1.5)
Katrenikona	4	2	0	0	0	0	0	6 (1.0)	6 (1.0)
Total	**19 (3.2)**	**14 (2.3)**	**2 (0.3)**	**5 (0.8)**	**2 (0.3)**	**5 (0.8)**	**0 (0.0)**	**47 (7.8)**	**47 (7.8)**

unhappy and 8 per cent felt very unhappy, regarding the rehabilitation facilities.

2. Respondents who felt very happy are among illiterates and respondents with primary level study (0.8 per cent each). Respondents who felt happy are more among illiterates (35 per cent), and respondents who felt unhappy are more among respondents with primary level study. Respondents who felt very unhappy are also more among illiterates (3.2 per cent).

3. The mandal-wise scenario shows that the respondents who felt very happy are more in Amalapuram mandal (1.3 per cent). Respondents, who felt happy are more in Katrenikona mandal (20 per cent), and respondents who felt satisfactory are also more in Amalapuram mandal (2 per cent), respondents who felt unhappy are more in Ainavilli mandal (11 per cent), and the respondents who felt very unhappy are more in Ambajipeta mandal (3 per cent).

4.

   (a) The opinions of illiterate respondents with regard to rehabilitation programmes show that more number felt happy (35 per cent).

   (b) The opinions of respondents with primary level education show that more number felt happy (11 per cent).

   (c) The opinions of respondents with upper primary education show that more number felt happy (5 per cent).

   (d) The opinions of respondents with secondary education show that more number felt unhappy (4 per cent).

   (e) The opinions of respondents with Inter qualification show that more number felt unhappy (2 per cent).

   (f) The opinions of respondents with Degree qualification show that equal number felt happy and unhappy (2 per cent each).

   (g) The opinions of respondents with other qualification show that more number felt happy (0.7 per cent).

5. Overall, majority felt happy (57 per cent) with regard to rehabilitation programmes. The

respondents with Secondary, Inter and Degree qualifications felt unhappy per cent with the programmes. The unhappiest respondents are more in Ambajipeta mandal.

Occupation: Opinions on Rehabilitation Facilities

In Table-5.9, Rehabilitation of respondents in relation to occupation is presented, based on which the following observations can be made:

1. Out of the total sample of 600 respondents, only 3 per cent felt very happy, majority (57 per cent) felt happy, 7 per cent felt satisfactory, 24 per cent felt unhappy and 8 per cent felt very unhappy regarding the rehabilitation facilities.
2. The respondents who felt very happy are more among the respondents who are in the field of

Table 5.9: Occupation: Opinion on Rehabilitation Facilities.

A: Agriculture B: Coconut plantation C: Private Job D: Government service E: Weaving F: Self-employment G: Fishing H: Service I: Agricultural Labour

Mandal	*Very Happy*									
	A	*B*	*C*	*D*	*E*	*F*	*G*	*H*	*I*	*TR*
Amalapuram	1	1	0	2	0	1	0	3	0	8 (1.3)
Ambajipeta	0	3	0	1	0	0	0	0	0	4 (0.7)
I. Polavaram	1	0	0	0	0	0	0	0	0	1 (0.2)
Ainavilli	4	1	0	0	0	0	0	0	0	5 (0.8)
Katrenikona	1	0	0	0	0	0	0	0	0	1 (0.2)
Total	**7 (1.2)**	**5 (0.8)**	**0 (0.0)**	**3 (0.5)**	**0 (0.0)**	**1 (0.2)**	**0 (0.0)**	**3 (0.5)**	**0 (0.0)**	**19 (3.2)**

(Table Contd...)

Table 5.9: Contd...

Mandal	*Happy*									
	A	*B*	*C*	*D*	*E*	*F*	*G*	*H*	*I*	*TR*
Amalapuram	0	5	2	3	11	2	0	1	3	27 (4.5)
Ambajipeta	2	4	1	3	1	0	0	1	17	29 (4.8)
I. Polavaram	25	9	1	3	0	4	29	2	17	91 (15.2)
Ainavilli	21	7	1	0	0	2	3	0	41	75 (12.5)
Katrenikona	47	4	0	1	0	2	38	3	27	122 (20.3)
Total	**96 (16.8)**	**29 (3.7)**	**5 (0.3)**	**10 (1.7)**	**12 (2.0)**	**10 (1.7)**	**70 (11.7)**	**7 (1.2)**	**105 (17.5)**	**344 (57.3)**

Table 5.9: Contd...

Mandal	*Satisfactory*									
	A	*B*	*C*	*D*	*E*	*F*	*G*	*H*	*I*	*TR*
Amalapuram	2	2	0	4	1	0	0	1	2	12 (2.0)
Ambajipeta	0	2	0	1	0	0	0	0	1	4 (0.7)
I. Polavaram	2	0	0	0	0	1	5	0	2	10 (1.7)
Ainavilli	3	1	0	0	0	0	0	1	3	8 (1.2)
Katrenikona	5	0	0	0	0	0	3	0	2	10 (1.7)
Total	**12 (2.0)**	**5 (0.8)**	**0 (0.0)**	**5 (0.8)**	**1 (0.2)**	**1 (0.2)**	**8 (1.3)**	**2 (0.3)**	**10 (1.7)**	**44 (7.3)**

Table 5.9: Contd...

Mandal	*Unhappy*									
	A	*B*	*C*	*D*	*E*	*F*	*G*	*H*	*I*	*TR*
Amalapuram	1	3	1	6	10	1	0	5	1	28 (4.7)
Ambajipeta	1	4	1	3	0	0	0	3	10	22 (3.7)

(Table Contd...)

Table 5.9: Contd...

Mandal	*Unhappy*									
	A	*B*	*C*	*D*	*E*	*F*	*G*	*H*	*I*	*TR*
I. Polavaram	14	1	0	1	0	3	5	0	2	26 (4.3)
Ainavilli	24	14	0	3	1	3	0	4	17	66 (11.0)
Katrenikona	1	0	0	0	0	0	3	0	0	4 (0.7)
Total	**41 (6.8)**	**22 (3.7)**	**2 (0.3)**	**13 (2.2)**	**11 (1.8)**	**7 (1.2)**	**8 (1.3)**	**12 (2.0)**	**30 (5.0)**	**146 (24.4)**

Table 5.9: Contd...

Mandal	*Very Unhappy*										Grand
	A	*B*	*C*	*D*	*E*	*F*	*G*	*H*	*I*	*TR*	*Total*
Amalapuram	3	0	0	2	2	0	0	0	3	10 (1.7)	85
Ambajipeta	2	4	0	2	0	0	0	1	10	19 (3.2)	75
I. Polavaram	2	0	0	0	0	0	1	0	0	3 (0.5)	131
Ainavilli	2	0	0	0	0	1	0	0	6	9 (1.5)	163
Katrenikona	2	0	0	0	0	0	4	0	0	6 (1.0)	143
Total	**11 (1.8)**	**4 (0.7)**	**0 (0.0)**	**4 (0.7)**	**2 (0.3)**	**1 (0.2)**	**5 (0.8)**	**1 (0.2)**	**19 (3.2)**	**47 (7.8)**	**600 (100.0)**

agriculture (2 per cent) and respondents who felt happy are also more among respondents who are in the field of agriculture (21 per cent). The respondents who felt satisfactory are more among the respondents who are also in the field of agriculture (2.8 per cent). The respondents who felt unhappy are also in the field of agriculture (11 per cent), followed by 5 per cent agriculture labourers. The respondents who felt very unhappy are more among agriculture labourers (3.2 per cent).

3. The mandal-wise scenario shows that the respondents who felt very happy are more in Amalapuram mandal (1.3 per cent). The respondents who felt happy are more in Katrenikone mandal (20 per cent). The respondents who felt satisfactory are also more in Amalapuram mandal (11 per cent). And the respondents who felt very unhappy are more in Ambajipeta mandal (3 per cent).

4.

(a) The opinions of the respondents who are in the field of agriculture with regard to rehabilitation programmes show that more number felt happy (21 per cent).

(b) The opinions of the respondents who are doing private jobs show that equal number felt very happy and happy (0.8 per cent each).

(c) The opinions of the respondents who are in Government jobs, show that, more number felt unhappy (2.2 per cent).

(d) The opinions of the respondents who are weavers show that more number felt happy (2 per cent), followed by 1.8 per cent who felt unhappy.

(e) The opinions of the respondents who are in self-employment show that more number (1.7 per cent) felt happy.

(f) The opinions of the respondents who are in fishing show that more number (12 per cent) felt happy.

(g) The opinions of the respondents who are doing service occupations show that more number (2 per cent) felt unhappy.

(h) The opinions of the respondents who are agricultural labourers, show that more number (18 per cent) felt happy.

5. Overall, majority of the respondents (57 per cent) felt happy with the programmes, while the unhappiest persons are in Ambajipeta mandal with 3 per cent. And coming to the occupations, Government servants, the respondents with service occupations and weavers felt unhappy with the said programmes.

Total Household Income: Opinions on Rehabilitation Facilities

In Table-5.10, Rehabilitation of the respondents in relation to total household income is presented based on which the following observations can be made(for table see at the end of the chapter).

Table 5.10: Total Household Income: Opinions on Rehabilitation Facilities.

A: 5000 B: 5000-15000 C: 15000-25000 D: 25000-35000 E: 35000-45000 F: 45000-55000 G: 55000-65000 TR: Total Respondents

Mandal	*Verty Happy*							
	A	*B*	*C*	*D*	*E*	*F*	*G*	*TR*
Amalapuram	0	4	1	1	0	0	2	8 (1.3)
Ambajipeta	0	0	0	2	0	0	2	4 (0.7)
I. Polavaram	0	1	0	0	0	0	0	1 (0.2)
Ainavilli	0	3	1	0	0	1	0	5 (0.8)
Katrenikona	1	0	0	0	0	0	0	1 (0.2)
Total	**1 (0.2)**	**8 (1.3)**	**2 (0.3)**	**3 (0.5)**	**0 (0.0)**	**1 (0.2)**	**4 (0.7)**	**19 (3.2)**

(Table Contd...)

Table 5.10: Contd...

Mandal	*Happy*							
	A	*B*	*C*	*D*	*E*	*F*	*G*	*TR*
Amalapuram	0	9	12	2	1	1	2	27 (4.5)
Ambajipeta	0	18	7	1	0	0	3	29 (4.8)
I. Polavaram	10	34	18	14	5	5	5	91 (15.2)
Ainavilli	4	49	15	3	2	2	0	75 (12.5)
Katrenikona	32	79	7	3	1	0	0	122 (20.3)
Total	**46 (7.7)**	**189 (31.5)**	**59 (9.8)**	**23 (3.8)**	**9 (1.5)**	**8 (1.3)**	**10 (1.7)**	**344 (57.3)**

Table 5.10: Contd...

Mandal	*Satisfactory*							
	A	*B*	*C*	*D*	*E*	*F*	*G*	*TR*
Amalapuram	1	6	1	1	0	0	3	12 (2.0)
Ambajipeta	0	3	0	0	0	0	1	4 (0.7)
I. Polavaram	1	6	3	0	0	0	0	10 (1.7)
Ainavilli	1	5	1	0	1	0	0	8 (1.2)
Katrenikona	2	7	1	0	0	0	0	10 (1.7)
Total	**5 (0.8)**	**27 (4.5)**	**6 (1.0)**	**1 (0.2)**	**1 (0.2)**	**0 (0.0)**	**4 (0.7)**	**44 (7.3)**

Table 5.10: Contd...

Mandal	*Unhappy*							
	A	*B*	*C*	*D*	*E*	*F*	*G*	*TR*
Amalapuram	1	11	7	2	3	0	5	28 (4.7)
Ambajipeta	0	16	1	0	0	0	5	22 (3.7)

(Table Contd...)

Table 5.10: Contd...

Mandal	*Unhappy*							
	A	*B*	*C*	*D*	*E*	*F*	*G*	*TR*
I. Polavaram	2	9	7	4	4	0	0	26 (4.3)
Ainavilli	0	48	8	6	1	1	2	66 (11.0)
Katrenikona	0	3	1	0	0	0	0	4 (0.7)
Total	**2 (0.3)**	**87 (14.5)**	**24 (2.0)**	**12 (2.0)**	**8 (1.3)**	**1 (0.2)**	**12 (2.0)**	**146 (24.4)**

Table 5.10: Contd...

Mandal	*Unhappy*								*Grand*
	A	*B*	*C*	*D*	*E*	*F*	*G*	*TR*	*Total*
Amalapuram	0	2	4	1	0	0	3	10 (1.7)	85
Ambajipeta	0	13	1	0	0	0	5	19 (3.2)	78
I. Polavaram	1	0	0	1	1	0	0	3 (0.5)	131
Ainavilli	0	7	2	0	0	0	0	9 (1.5)	163
Katrenikona	0	6	0	0	0	0	0	6 (1.0)	143
Total	**1 (0.2)**	**28 (4.7)**	**7 (1.2)**	**2 (0.3)**	**1 (0.2)**	**0 (0.0)**	**8 (1.3)**	**47 (7.8)**	**600 (100.0)**

1. Out of the total sample of 600 respondents, only 3 per cent felt very happy, 57 per cent happy, 7 per cent felt satisfactory, 24 per cent felt unhappy and 8 per cent felt very unhappy regarding the rehabilitation facilities.

2. The respondents who felt very happy are more among Rs.5,000-15,000 income group. The respondents who felt happy are also more among Rs.5,000-15,000 income group. The respondents who felt satisfactory are also more among Rs.5,000-15,000 income group. The respondents

who felt unhappy are also more among Rs.5,000-15,000 income group. The respondents who felt very unhappy are also more among the Rs.5,000-15,000 income group.

3. The mandal-wise scenario shows that the respondents who felt very happy are more in Amalapuram mandal (1.3 .per cent). The respondents who felt happy are more in Katrenikone mandal (20 per cent). The respondents who felt satisfactory are also more in Amalapuram mandal (2 per cent). The respondents who felt unhappy are more in Ainavilli mandal (11 per cent). And the respondents who felt very unhappy are more in Ambajipeta mandal (3 per cent).

4.

(a) The opinions of the respondents in the low income group (Rs.<5,000-15,000) with regard to rehabilitation programmes show that more number felt happy (40 per cent).

(b) The opinions of the respondents in the middle income groups (Rs.15,000-45,000) with regard to rehabilitation programmes show that more number felt (15 per cent) happy.

(c) The opinions of the respondents who are in high income group show that more number felt happy (3 per cent) followed by 2.2 per cent who felt unhappy.

(d) Emphasising total household income, there is no much variation in the opinions of low, middle and high income groups, with regard to rehabilitation programmes.

6

Summary and Suggestions

Summary

India having a long coastline of over 8,000 km has a variety of natural coastal ecosystems. The coastal stretches of peninsular India are much prone to cyclones that originate in the Bay of Bengal and the Arabian Sea. The Ocean depressions coupled with North-East and South-West monsoons cause much devastation to the coastal economic zone. Such a natural calamity generally takes place during August-November in a year.

Andhra Pradesh is India's third largest State with a population of 66 millions (1991 census) larger than most nations. Almost half of the population of Andhra Pradesh live in the eight districts of the coastal belt. The Coastal Districts of Andhra Pradesh experience such a devastation almost every year due to its geographical position in relation to the Bay of Bengal, ocean currents and wind paths. The entire coastal stretch gets hit by cyclones and their allied natural phenomena like deltas of the Rivers Godavari, Krishna and Pennar which are much prone to great losses both in terms of lives and materials. Since the delta region lies low with monotonous landscape, the low magnitude and cyclones cause much devastation. The deltas of the coastal region are providing two eco-niches such as aquatic and inland resources. The former resource is exploited by the fishing communities, and the latter by the agrarian communities. The settlements of the fishing population are located very contiguous to the coast. Annually one or two cyclonic storms either hit or skirt the Andhra coast, some in April-May and in September-December with October and November being statistically the critical months. The most vulnerable coast districts are Prakasam, Guntur, Krishna, West Godavari and East Godavari. These are all low lying and most of the mandals contain heavily populated delta areas. A storm surge is likely to sweep inland if it strikes any of these districts and they are also subject to flooding from inland rain.

Statement of the Problem

In reckoning of the recent cyclone devastation on the East Coast of Andhra Pradesh, it is proposed to undertake a sociological survey on the effects of cyclone. The study examines sociogical, social, psychological and economical conditions of East Godavari District before and after the impact of cyclone that has occurred during 6th -8th, November 1996. For all practical purposes, this study will be referred to as "Cyclone Devastation in Andhra Pradesh."

The cyclone storm crossed the coast at Kakinada at 10.30 p.m. about 50 kms in North-West direction on the 6th day of November. Despite of all steps taken by the authorities, the storm has devasted both Central and Eastern deltas in the district in an unprecedented manner. Thousands of trees were uprooted, thatched houses have been completely damaged and the entire socio-economic infrastructure has been damaged.

Study Area

The study is conducted in one of the coastal districts of Andhra Pradesh viz., East Godavari, one of the most vulnerable coastal districts which is subjected to frequent spell of cyclones rooted in the Bay of Bengal.

Objectives of the Study

1. To ascertain the natural extent and magnitude of the devastation caused by the November 1996 cyclone.
2. To analyse the sociological, social, psychological and economical aspects of the study area before and after the impact of cyclone.
3. To assess the rehabilitation programmes extended by the Government and the NGOs.
4. To assess the attitude of the beneficiaries towards the implementation of rehabilitation and reconstruction programmes.
5. To assess the attitudes of the Government and the NGOs towards the same programmes.
6. To suggest modifications, if any, in the said programmes to achieve well-desired social transformation.
7. To investigate and record carefully all the perceptions and reactions of the affected (survival victims) people during the field study.

Methodology

The rationale of the study in confining to East Godavari District is that the cyclonic storm crossed the coast at the South of Kakinada, the district headquarters and caused heavy damages to kacha/semi-permanent houses and crops, resulting in huge losses of life and property and disruption of communication lines and electricity supply in almost all the mandals in the district.

Out of the five Revenue Divisions in East Godavari District, Amalapuram Revenue Division is selected for study. The rationality of selecting this Revenue Division is again that the extent of damage is more in Amalapuram

Division than in other four Divisions in terms of damage to lives and property (see Table-1.2 and Table-1.3).

In Amalapuram Revenue Division, out of 16 mandals, five mandals are selected for study based on the extent of damage to lives and property. The selected five mandals are Amalapuram, Ambajipeta, I. Polavaram, Ainavilli and Katrenikona. In Amalapuram mandal, out of 18 villages, three villages are selected for study. In Ambajipeta mandal, out of 13 villages, three villages are selected for study. In I. Polavaram mandal, out of 11 villages, five villages are selected for study. In Ainavilli mandal, out of 17 villages, six villages are selected for study and in Katrenikona mandal, out of 14 villages, seven villages are selected for study. According to the Notification of the Collector, East Godavari District, the total 215 villages in Amalapuram Revenue Division are severely affected with more than 75 per cent damage.

The selection of the villages is based on random sampling. Every sixth village in Amalapuram mandal is selected for study. Every fourth village in Ambajipeta mandal is selected. In the same way, every second village in I. Polavaram mandal every third village in Ainavilli mandal and every second village in Katrenikona mandal are selected for study. The size of the sample is 600 and the total respondents are purposively selected depending upon the damage, availability, and responsiveness of the respondents in each village.

The data are collected by pre-designed schedule consisting of structured and open-end questions administered through interviews. The schedule consists of questions with regard to: (a) respondent's personal details (like age, marital status, literacy level, caste, religion, occupation, income level), (b) household particulars (like sex composition, number of earning members, their literacy, occupation, income levels), (c) extent of damage to lives, property and crops, (d) time taken to restore to original position (both financial and psychological), (e) life styles, living and psychological conditions before during and after cyclone, (f) opinions of the respondents with regard to adequacy of rehabilitation programmes at the time of and after cyclone conducted by the Central and the State and Voluntary Organizations, (g) the extent of damage and restoration of their villages in the words of respondents, (h) politicization of relief and rehabilitation effort. Using the schedule, the data are collected from 600 respondents by the field investigators.

The collected data are structured in case with open-ended questions and then coded and tabulated using computer.

Limitations

Any social study has its own limitations and this fact is applicable to this study also.

1. The first limitation is the selection of villages and respondents. The size of the sample in each village is not uniform because it is very difficult for the field investigators to do random selection of affected respondents. Convenience, the intensity of the problem, and the openness of the respondents are taken into account in the selection of villages and respondents.

2. Another limitation is that comparison can be made when there is previous economic status with that of the extent of damage done due to cyclone. This point is missing in this study.

3. Migration another important social factor is also not included.

4. Comparisons can also be done like affected respondents with that of unaffected respondents

in the same places of affected mandals (Revenue Divisions) with that of un-affects mandals.

5. Even though the interview Schedule which is meant for collecting data, is prepared exhaustively; the investigators are unable to procure data with regard to some variables.

In spite of the limitations; the study throws a new light through sampling techniques which are so far absent in this type of studies. Further, the study broadens the path to new researchers to explore further and this study is an eye-opener for the Government in the mitigation of natural disasters.

Profile of the Study Area

The selected district, East Godavari is one among the 10 coastal districts of Andhra Pradesh (1991 census). The district has a coastline of 161 km. The population of the district is 45,41,220 as per 1991 census which is 6.8 per cent of the total population of the State. It is the most populous district in Andhra Pradesh. Out of the total population, males constitute 22,72,962 and females 22,68,260 with a sex ratio of 998 females per 1000 males. It consists of five Revenue Divisions. Out of the five Revenue Divisions, there are 59 mandals. It has a total coast-line of 117 km., and most of the mandals in the district are vulnerable to cyclone and consequential heavy rains.

Amalapuram Revenue Division is one among the five Revenue Divisions in East Godavari District. The division is an island surrounded by water on all its sides. The Gowthami Godavari River lies to its North, the Bay of Bengal is to its Eastern and Southern sides while the Vasista River is to its Western side. It is also known as “Konaseema”, which means the land situated at the terminus. The geographical area of the division is 3,83,176 acres (1,550.66 sq. km.), out of which the net area sown during kharif (1999-2000) is 2,59,239 acres. The total population of the division is 11,23,922 as per 1991 census, out of which there are 5,60,540 male and 5,63,382 are females. The division consists of 3,10,595 (27.6 per cent) Scheduled Castes and 6,941 (0.6 per cent) Scheduled Tribe population.

Previous history of natural calamities in Amalapuram Revenue Division

Amalapuram Revenue Division experienced two severe floods (one in 1953 and another in 1986) and three cyclones (1969, 1977 and 1996). Another natural hazard from ground is called 'ONGC Blow-out' (also known as, Pasarlapudi Blow-out) in the year 1995.

6th-7th November, 1996 Cyclone

A cyclone storm started in the Bay of Bengal on 5th November, 1996. It continued on a Westerly course on 6th November, 1996 dramatically picked up speed and moved in a West-North-Westerly direction and crossed the Andhra Coast at about 10.30 p.m. on the intervening night of 6th/ 7th November, 1996. At the time of the landfall, the wind speed recorded was of the order of 120 knots (221 kms/ Hour). Hence, the cyclone was of a very severe intensity.

Profile of the Respondents

The present chapter deals exclusively with the socio-economic characteristics of the respondents. It is divided into Two Parts. Part-A presents the personal profile of respondents. Part-B presents the household profile of respondents.

Looking at the overall data on the socio-economic structure of the respondents, the following conclusions can be made: The socio-economic data of the respondents indicates predominance of Hindu. The caste structure of the respondents denotes that 38 per cent of the respondents belong to Backward Castes, followed by Forward Castes with 34 per cent, Scheduled Castes with 27 per cent and a small minority of Scheduled Tribes. The sample consists of 95 per cent of male respondents and 5 per cent female respondents. The reason for the predominance of the male respondents is that of a patriarchal nature of society wherein usually the head of the household is a male member. The data consists of 95 per cent male married respondents which is coterminous with Indian family structure which is mostly patrilineal. Majority (56 per cent) of the respondents are in their middle age (30-49) and the mean age of the respondents is 46.3. The literacy levels of the respondents show that a little less than half are significantly illiterate; one-fourth of the respondents have studied upto primary level and only 8 per cent of the total sample have good academic background. The occupational structure of the respondents reveals that being Konaseema the sample consists of 39 per cent of landholders. Significantly a little more than one-fourth are agricultural labourers. It shows that 66 per cent of the respondents are dependent on agriculture and the devastating impact of cyclone varies from cultivator to agricultural labourer. Next, fishing is another major occupation of the respondents. The income levels of the respondents shows that nearly 80 per cent are with low income and only 7 per cent belong to highest income groups. The mean size of the income of the respondents is Rs.14,283.3.

The household particulars of respondents reveal that majority are living in nuclear families with three to four family members. The mean size of the household is 3.9 members. The sex composition of the household is favourable to male members. Half of the households have 2-3 earning members. The literacy levels of the household show that significant numbers are illiterate (41 per cent).

The occupational structure of the household is same to that of the respondents with predominance of agriculture and fishing. The economic scenario shows that majority of the households belongs to low income groups. The mean size of the total household income is Rs.17,095.8.

Damage Assessment

Due to the severe cyclonic storm which crossed the coast, South of Kakinada with gale winds of 120 knots, there were heavy damages to crops, coconut plantations, and houses, resulting in huge losses to life and property and with disruption of communication lines and electricity supply in almost all mandals in the district. In the Introductory Chapter, the damage assessment is presented based on the Revenue Divisions in East Godavari District. The devastation data of the selected mandals in the Amalapuram Revenue Division are given in the profile of the Study Area. In this chapter, the extent of damages in the selected mandals are being presented and analysed while using the primary data and the overall devastation scenario of the district using the East Godavari District Collector's Notification.

The chapter is divided into three Parts. Part-A presents the extent of damage to lives and property. Part-B explains the restoration of the respondents and in Part-C, the rescue operations, and the adequacy of Rehabilitation facilities are discussed based on the opinions of the respondents.

While summarizing the data in Part-A, which deals with the extent of damage to lives and property the following observations can be made. The sample denotes that 166 deaths occurred on the whole and majority of deaths (94 cases) were reported in I. Polavaram mandal followed by Katrenikona and Ainavilli mandals. The extent of damage to property in the selected mandals is

Rs.35,705,870. As a matter of fact, the extent of damage to landed property is more (54 per cent) as the area is famous for coconuts and paddy followed by 42 per cent damage to residential houses and 4 per cent damage to livestock. While taking the statistics of damage to crops, it is considered that coconut plants are badly affected with 56 per cent damage followed by 35 per cent damage to paddy with Vegetables and Banana crops also getting affected in these areas.

Coming to Part-B, the summary of restoration position of respondents as observed by the researcher is as follows: On the whole, 71.5 per cent of the total sample told that they are restored to their original positions, and 28.5 per cent said they are not yet restored. Majority (45 per cent) took 3-6 months to get restored and 37 per cent took one to two years and even more to restore themselves from the cyclone devastation. Majority of the respondents (34 per cent) spent Rs.10,000-20,000 to repair their damages to their property, and a significant number (15 per cent) spent Rs.50,000 and more. A little more than half of the respondents spent less than Rs.10,000 from their own finances towards restoration. Nearly half of the respondents spent less than Rs.10,000 from the sources of loans. Half of the respondents spent Rs.10,000-20,000 towards restoration from the above two sources. All the respondents said they got aid from the authorities with the amounts varying from respondent to respondent depending upon the extent of damage. But, it is paradoxical that the Central and the State assistance including those of voluntary organizations concentrated on the severely affected areas and poured funds accordingly. This is also one of the reasons for the variations of aid. Anyhow, majority (37 per cent) of the respondents got aid worth Rs.700-1100 and 14 per cent got the highest amounts in the severely affected mandals wherein more deaths took place.

The respondents' opinions about the productivity of crops show that half of the respondents were partly satisfied and 30 per cent of them were dissatisfied with the yields of their crops after the cyclone. After the cyclone, a little more than half of the respondents felt scarcity of money. The respondents also felt scarcity of food, clothing, water, medicines and other necessary items after the cyclone. Nearly half of the respondents felt that the living conditions are very bad after the cyclone. Majority of the respondents (85 per cent) expressed that their psychological condition were very fearful during the cyclone and even after the cyclone, while a significant number (15 per cent) expressed that still the miserable experiences of that day are haunting their minds. Most of the respondent (38 per cent) opined that nothing can be done about the cyclone while others held the opinions like cyclone is a curse and it a natural thing. Only a minority (7 per cent) opined that it can be managed to some extent.

Part-C deals with rescue and rehabilitation programmes. Majority of the respondents (59 per cent) felt that the State government came to their rescue during the cyclone. A significant number (29 per cent) opined that their close relatives came to their rescue during the cyclone, which shows that majority of the people in the affected areas did not get immediate help from the authorities, and which might be one of the reasons for their dissatisfaction with regard to rescue operations.

A little more than half of the respondents expressed their satisfaction with regard to the rescue operations of the State and by the efforts of the voluntary organizations after the cyclone. Especially, in the selected mandals of Katrenikona and Ainavilli, services and money provided by the voluntary organizations were really laudable, in the words of respondents. All the respondents received monetary help from the authorities after the cyclone, though the amount varie from mandal to mandal as there was lack of coordination among the officials and the voluntary organizations. Majority of respondents did not get the necessary items like medicines, food grains, kerosene, clothes etc., after the cyclone. Even the then R.D.O. of Amalapuram Revenue Division also expressed his inability to provide food, drinking water, accommodation and shelter, because the relief camps got flooded with people by more than their capacities, as there was total devastation and havoc in the entire area. In Amalapuram Revenue Division, 333 relief camps were organized for a total number of 1,33,702 evacuees. Majority (65 per cent) of the respondents opined that the rescue operations are adequate, whereas, 35 per cent of them told that they experienced inadequate rescue operations. Majority of the respondents (87 per cent) cited that funds were insufficient, 31 per cent felt that there were undue delays in the rehabilitation facilities and the other cited reasons were about the deficiencies of Rehabilitation, come from lack of commitment among the officials, lack of co-ordination among the Central and State Governments and voluntary organizations, among whom traces of corruption and favouritism among the officials were bound. On the whole, a little more than half of the respondents expressed their happiness towards the rehabilitation facilities.

Restoration and Rehabilitation are the most important key variables in the study of natural disasters, which occur too infrequently to warrant (or force) a great expenditure of money, attention or managerial expertise. On the whole, it seems that many governments are not in fact capable of providing an efficient response to a natural disaster any more than they can ameliorate or prevent man-made disaster, or deliver basic services (health, shelter, food) to their populations (Stephen, P. Cohen & C.V. Raghavulu, 1979).

The restoration of the affected people depends upon how best the authorities provide rescue and rehabilitation programmes, besides individual effort. Eavacuation or rescue, in the case of cyclones, requires near-perfect information as well as an efficient system of population movement, to safer places or relief camps. In this context, respondent's caste, age, literacy level, occupation and household income are taken for analysis and presented through cross-tables in two sections.

Out of the 600 respondents, majority are restored (71.5 per cent) and only 28.5 per cent are not-restored: (i) Out of 600, more number of restored (25 per cent) belonged to backward castes, followed by forward castes (24 per cent) and scheduled castes (22 per cent). (ii) More number of not-restored respondents also belong to backward castes (12 per cent), followed by forward castes (10 per cent) and 5 per cent in case of scheduled castes. (iii) On the whole also, backward caste respondents are more with 38 per cent, followed by 34 per cent forward caste respondents and 27 per cent scheduled caste respondents. More number of backward caste respondents are not-restored, compared to other groups.

Out of the total 600 sample, majority (71 per cent) are restored and only 28.5 per cent are not-restored. (i) Out of the total 600, more number of restored respondents are middle-aged (42 per cent), followed by the respondents in the age-group of 50-59 (13 per cent) and old aged (13 per cent) (ii) More number of not-restored respondents are also middle-aged (14 per cent) followed by old-aged respondents (7 per cent) and 6 per cent in 50-59 age-group. (iii) On the whole, middle-aged (56 per cent) are in majority in the total sample, followed by 19 per cent 50-59 age-group, with a significant number 18 per cent old aged respondents. (i) In comparison, we can say that more number of restored respondents are middle-aged. (ii) More number of young-aged (out of total 44 in the age-group of 20-29) are not-restored.

(i) Out of the total 600 respondents restored respondents (68 per cent) are illiterates, the restored respondents with high academic qualifications are 5 per cent. (ii) More number of not-restored are illiterates (16 per cent) followed by 6 per cent of primary level respondents. The not-restored respondents with high academic qualifications are only 3 per cent. (iii) On the whole, literates (53 per cent) topped the total sample of 600. The primary level (44 per cent) respondents are more among the literates. (iv) In comparison, the literates, that too, more with high academic qualifications, are restored more. There is close association between literacy levels and restoration.

(i) Out of the 600 total size of the sample more number (30 per cent) are in the field of agriculture, followed by agricultural labour (19 per cent) and fishing (10 per cent). (ii) More number of not-restored (9 per cent) are also in the field of agriculture, followed by agricultural labour (8 per cent) and fishing (5 per cent). (iii) Except the respondents in Government service and in all other fields, restored are more than not-restored. (iv) Relatively more number of Government servants are not-restored. (v) And half of the respondents, as fishing as their major occupation, are not-restored. It is quite natural that agricultural labourers and fishermen, who belonged to low income groups are not-restored.

Out of 600 total size of the sample, majority are restored (71.5 per cent), (i) Out of 600, 38 per cent who are restored belonged to Rs.5000-15000 income group and 18 per cent of not-restored also belonged to Rs.5000-15000 income group. (ii) Compared to restored and not-restored respondents, the restored respondents are more in low and middle income groups, but interestingly the comparative figure is more in not-restored respondents in high income groups (3.8 per cent to 4.1 per cent). But, there is no much relation between total household income and restoration.

Out of the total sample of 600 respondents, only 3 per cent felt very happy, 5 per cent felt happy, 7 per cent felt satisfactory, 24 per cent felt unhappy and 8 per cent felt very unhappy regarding the rehabilitation facilities. The mandal-wise scenario shows that, respondents, who felt very happy, are more in Amalapuram mandal (1.3 per cent). The respondents who felt happy, are more in Katrenikona mandal (20 per cent). The respondents, who felt satisfactory, are also more in Amalapuram mandal (2 per cent). The respondents, who felt unhappy, are more in Ainavilli mandal (11 per cent). And the respondents, who felt very unhappy, are more in Ambajipeta mandal (3 per cent). The respondents with Secondary, Inter and Degree qualifications felt unhappy per cent with the programmes. And coming to the occupations, Government servants, the respondents with service occupations and weavers felt unhappy with the said programmes.

Suggestions

1. Enumeration is the most important aspect of Damage assessment. It should be done impartially authentically, rationally and immediately after the cyclone without lapse of time. It is not merely meant for giving compensation to the affected people, but it should aim at giving moral boosting and support to genuine victims, viz; farmers and fishermen, who are hit by the cyclone badly. Wrong official data or wrong enumeration produce or result in wrong estimations, which further cause grave injustice to the affected, also spreading unrest and dissatisfaction among the people. This might be one of the reasons for the unhappiness of respondents with regard to rehabilitation facilities.
2. As per the knowledge of the respondents, there were many lapses. Many respondents cited that they didn't get the full ex gratia amounts as announced by the Government.

3. In the case of missing persons also, the respondents are at a loss to know about their fate, this should be studied further.
4. Even though people should be motivated towards taking effective steps and not waiting for the officials to do every thing, as mentioned by the officials, it is difficult to send messages to interior places in-time. In such cases, the dynamic youth in those places are motivated to evacuate the innocent people to safer places, in order to reduce the death toll. In that regard, education and mass-media play a major role in moulding the character of the people.
5. Further, the worst-hit people are the fishermen community, who depend on the sea and live nearby the sea. So, the chances of damage to their lives is very high. Permanent cyclone rehabilitation centres should be provided in all interior coastal areas and should be maintained properly. If not, in times of necessity and need those centres will not be in a position to support the affected people. Studies reflect that poverty rate is very high in those communities and steps should be taken to reduce poverty, so that the younger generation may be in a position to take advantage of educational facilities and can be aware of their problems and solutions.
6. Above all, people's motivation is a must in mitigating the impact of natural calamities and steps should be taken in that direction.
7. There should be co-operation among Government officials and personnel from voluntary organizations in keeping up after-cyclone services. Some areas got poured with money and other basic materials, while some other areas faced paucity of assistance and resources.

Sociological Implications of the Study

1. People living in Low-lying areas are very much afraid and are in a state of fear to encounter even a small drizzle or rain.
2. Majority of the victims of cyclone have developed apathy for raising plantations (especially, growing big trees) in front of their houses.
3. All the survivors of the cyclone are brought under one platform in sharing their grief together, thereby getting relief from a neighbouhood feeling.
4. There are cases of individual householders, when death of every one in the family, except himself made a respondent shockingly alone and making him incompetent to face life single-handedly.
5. The cyclone made every dweller most exhausted, weak and diffident, leading to psychotraumatic maladjustments, even bringing premature deaths in certain cases.
6. The cyclone has since forced some of the victims to leave their places of birth, for good.
7. The cyclone led the social status of individuals and the families to a downward trend, with most of the small farmers getting manginalised.
8. Measures of rehabilitation, rescue and relief transformed some villages into new restructured entities.
9. The cyclone disaster made some individuals and families disorganized, which could not be restored to their original status, so as to join the main-stream of societal relationships.
10. During cyclone, there were instances of some people showering humanity upon the victims, during the ongoing rescue operations.

REFERENCES

1. Stephen P. Cohen & Raghavulu, C.V., 1979. The Andhra Cyclone of 1977, Individual and Institutional Responses to mass Death, Vikas Publishing House Pvt. Ltd., New Delhi.
2. Rashtriya Barh Ayog, 1980. National Commission on floods vol-1, Government of India, New Delhi.
3. David L. Sills, 1972. International Encyclopedia of the Social Sciences vol.3, the Macmillan Company, New York.
4. Baburao Naidu, T., 2000. My Experience with Hurricane, V.G.S. Publishers, Vijayawada.
5. Collector's Brief Note on Cyclone Storm, November 1996 in East Godavari District, Kakinada.
6. Indian Express, 8 November 1996.
7. Andhra Patrika (T) 9 November 1996.
8. Eenadu (T) 9 November 1996.
9. Deccon Cronicle 9 November 1996.
10. The Hindu 10 November 1996.